How to Write
SHORT
STORIES
for Magazines

– and get published!

How to Write
SHORT
STORIES
for Magazines
— and get published!

SOPHIE KING

oks

This book is dedicated to my children William, Lucy and Giles as well as all my creative writing students and fiction editors.

Published by How To Books Ltd,
Spring Hill House, Spring Hill Road,
Begbroke, Oxford OX5 1RX. United Kingdom.
Tel: (01865) 375794. Fax: (01865) 379162.
info@howtobooks.co.uk
www.howtobooks.co.uk

How To Books greatly reduce the carbon footprint of their books by sourcing their typesetting and printing in the UK.

British Library Cataloguing in Publication Data
A catalogue record for this book is available from the British Library

ISBN 978 1 84528 280 6

Photograph of author on page x by Jerry Baeur
Produced for How To Books by Deer Park Productions, Tavistock, Devon
Typeset by PDQ Typesetting, Newcastle-under-Lyme, Staffs.
Printed and bound by The Cromwell Press, Trowbridge, Wiltshire

NOTE: The material contained in this book is set out in good faith for general guidance and no liability can be accepted for loss or expense incurred as a result of relying in particular circumstances on statements made in the book. The laws and regulations are complex and liable to change, and readers should check the current position with the relevant authorities before making personal arrangements.

Contents

Preface

I started writing short stories about eight years ago, after hearing a talk by Gaynor Davies, fiction editor of *Woman's Weekly*. Until then, I had concentrated on being a journalist and a would-be novelist. However, I went home, wrote a story and sent it to Gaynor. To my delight, she accepted it and I haven't looked back. I love writing short stories although I've since had three novels published: *The School Run, Mums@Home, Second Time Lucky* and *The Supper Club* which is to be published in August (all published by Hodder & Stoughton).

I enjoy finding unusual angles for my stories and I'm always getting ideas at unexpected times. There's a real buzz in bringing it all to a conclusion in 800–2,000 words. Getting a short story published isn't easy but I've discovered that there are some definite Dos and Don'ts which increase (or decrease) your chances. Hopefully, my book will help you find the way.

Good luck!

About the author

Sophie King is the pen name of Jane Bidder who has been a journalist for over 25 years and contributes regularly to national newspapers and magazines including *The Daily Telegraph* and *Woman.* She writes novels under the name Sophie King, and her three previous books *The School Run*, *Mums@Home* and *Second Time Lucky* (published by Hodder & Stoughton) were described as best-sellers. Her latest novel, *The Supper Club* (also published by Hodder & Stoughton) is about four groups of friends who take it in turns to have monthly supper parties.

Sophie has had hundreds of short stories published in magazines such as *Woman's Weekly*, *Take a Break*, *My Weekly* and *Best*. She was the winner of the Elizabeth Goudge Short Story Trophy in 2005, as well as a runner up in the Harry Bowling Prize. She is a member of the Romantic Novelists Association, Women in Journalism, the Society of Women Writers and Journalists and the National Union of Journalists. She lectures in creative writing for Oxford University and West Herts College and is writer in residence at HMP Grendon.

For more details about Sophie and her work visit www.sophieking. info

1

Identifying Your Market

So you want to write short stories for magazines. Fine. But what kind of short stories? And what kind of magazines?

Many would-be short-story writers fail to achieve their ambition of getting published because they don't carry out some simple research. They presume that all short stories are the same because of their length which is . . . short!

Or they make the mistake of assuming that one woman's magazine is very like another with, of course, the odd difference here and there.

As a matter of interest, I wonder if you've checked in a newsagent's recently to see which magazines still run short stories nowadays? Sadly, some magazines have cut their fiction page. Luckily, the good news is that others are expanding them and also running monthly fiction specials with plenty of scope for good writing.

There are also other magazines which you might not have thought of or indeed known about, which also run short stories. I'll be giving you details about those later in the chapter.

FIRST STEP – GET AN IDEAS BOOK!
The first thing I teach my students is to buy themselves an 'Ideas

Book'. By this, I don't mean a spiral notebook like a reporter's pad. I mean a large, brightly coloured book which you won't lose. At the same time, buy yourself a pretty, coloured, small notebook for your handbag.

Use these to write down all your ideas for short stories so you won't forget them. Ideas can come at the most inconvenient times, can't they? When you're having a bath or driving or about to drift off to sleep.

You will probably think (as I used to) that your idea is so good that you won't forget it. But ideas are like cobwebs. They often float off, out of reach and it's so hard to remember them again.

So the golden rule is to write them down as soon as they occur to you. In your Ideas Book naturally.

There's more of this in the next chapter on Ideas. But it's so important, I wanted you to be aware of this right from the beginning.

STUDYING THE MAGAZINE MARKET

Getting a short story published is not easy. But you can maximise your chances by doing as much research as possible into the magazines which still publish fiction.

The first step is to buy as many magazines as you can or see if you can get them at the local library. Take time to have a good read. You'll be extremely surprised at how many different styles there are.

Some magazines have different kinds of stories within one issue. You might find that the same edition will have a serial with a feel-good tone to it and also a single-page short story with a twist in the tale at the end. There might also be a DPS (which means double page spread) story as well.

It's only by studying these magazines that you can get a feel for what kind of story you want to write and which publication you'd like to try your hand at. You also need to look at the magazines over a period of some weeks to get a proper flavour of their style, content and tone.

TARGETING SPECIFIC READERS

This is crucial if you're going to maximise your chances of success. A story which centres around a retired couple might not appeal to a magazine aimed at a younger readership.

On the other hand, it could work for another magazine like *Yours* or *The People's Friend* which has a wide age range of readers.

If your story has a risqué theme, it might not go down so well with a traditional magazine. Similarly, a conventional setting might not inspire a magazine aimed at twenty somethings.

Don't make the mistake of thinking that your story is so good that a fiction editor might bend the rules. It doesn't work that way! A fiction editor will be very aware of what works for his or her magazine and is looking for a story that fits into these guidelines.

HOW TO TELL WHAT A MAGAZINE WANTS

I've already advised you to study each magazine carefully. But don't merely turn to the fiction page. Take a good look at the rest of the publication too.

What kind of features does it run? What are they about? What kind of age range do you think they'll appeal to? Is it for home-lovers or working mums or both? Is it for grandparents or young couples?

It stands to reason that the fiction page has to fit in with the rest of the magazine so take your cue from the content.

Similarly, go through the adverts. Adverts can tell you a lot about the readership. Companies pay a lot of money for ads so they'll have made sure that these fit the readership profile. So if you are trying to place a story about a young couple, it might not suit a magazine with several ads for stair lifts!

OBTAINING MAGAZINE GUIDELINES

If you're already feeling confused, don't be! To make life easier, most magazines have their own set of fiction guidelines which you can either download from the internet or request by post.

These will tell you what kind of stories the fiction editor is looking for – and what he or she isn't looking for.

Of course, the requirements can change from month to month and these might not always be updated. But it does give you a general idea.

At the end of this chapter, I've reproduced some guidelines from well-known magazines on the market. It's important to read these well and see how it might affect your writing. You might have to have a re-think! For example, you will see that stories where the characters solve their problems by winning the lottery, usually get rejected.

Similarly, fiction editors aren't normally impressed if the character wakes up and finds it was all a dream. And beware of writing an ending where the character is actually a dog or rabbit – another favourite.

STORY LENGTH

Always make sure that your short story fits the required length. Over or underwriting is one of the most common reasons for stories being rejected. Fiction editors don't always have time to cut. Besides, if they've asked for 1,000 words, that's what they want – no matter how good you think your story is.

Of course it's hard to cut your work. We all hate doing it. But the funny thing is that once you start, you often end up with a story which is so much better because it's more concise and flows more smoothly. Try it and see!

Below are some guidelines on lengths for different magazines. You'll see that certain publications like *Best*, just run one page stories of between 1,000 and 1,200 words. Others like *The People's Friend* might run to over 2,000 words.

EXERCISE

Make a list of ideas for a possible short story.

Now take four magazines. Look through the features, letters page, advertisements and everything else inside. What kind of reader is it aimed at, in your view? Make a list of characteristics such as age, interests, sex, family, etc.

Would your ideas suit any of those magazines? Make a list of ideas and magazines which might match. Write these down in your Ideas Book.

EXAMPLES OF MAGAZINE GUIDELINES

Please note that these were correct at the time of going to press

My Weekly's New Fiction guidelines

All manuscripts must be typewritten, double spaced with accurate wordage supplied. You can send them your work by e-mail to myweekly@dcthomson.co.uk or by post to The Fiction Editor, *My Weekly*, D. C. Thomson & Co. Ltd, 80 Kingsway East, Dundee DD4 8SL.

Most important!
For your manuscript to be read and considered, it's imperative you mark prominently on your envelope or e-mail into which category your story falls. If you don't do this, your work can't be considered.

What are the required categories?
You'll find *My Weekly*'s present requirements below; not only the types but the lengths and the TV or films that could inspire your ideas.

Will the categories remain the same?
No, they will change as stocks fill up in some areas and deplete in others. Therefore, if you have an idea that doesn't suit *My Weekly*'s present requirements, don't despair. It may do so in the future. However, please be guided by the wordage mentioned.

How will I know when the categories have changed?
That's simple, you can phone (01382 575546) to check for any changes, or request the latest guidelines by post (please enclose an SAE) or by e-mail, or access *My Weekly*'s website.

Well, here are the details you're anxiously waiting for, so get your thinking caps on and good luck!

Do's and dont's

Dos
✓ Display clear intent.
✓ Be uplifting, have a message of hope.
✓ Offer different points of view.
✓ Have strong central characters.
✓ Be evocative and atmospheric, use light and shade.
✓ Use natural, modern dialogue.
✓ Portray relationships realistically.
✓ Introduce humour where appropriate.
✓ Try to move the reader.
✓ Uphold family values.
✓ Check all facts are accurate.
✓ Set stories in other countries.

Dont's
✗ Use black humour.
✗ Describe graphic violence.

✗ Construct stand-up humour.

✗ Rely on continuous one-liners.

✗ Include overt sexuality or smuttiness.

✗ Rely on formulaic predictability.

✗ Construct contrived storylines.

✗ Overlook punctuation/spelling and grammar.

✗ Use unrealistic dialogue/thoughts for a specific age groups.

✗ Portray one-dimensional characters.

✗ Use clichéd situations and dialogue.

✗ Neglect continuity.

Lengths

Short read: 800 words or less

♦ A moment in time.

♦ Misleading narrator.

♦ Character studies monologues.

♦ Unusual, offbeat subject.

♦ Humorous.

♦ Conversation – all dialogue.

Your inspiration

Alan Bennett, Radio 4 play, P. G. Wodehouse, Victoria Wood monologues, Roald Dahl's *Tales of the Unexpected*, *The Twilight Zone* (new version), 'Talking Heads' series.

Medium read: 1,300 or 2,000 words

♦ Could be one concept explored.

♦ Sting in the tail/surprise ending.

♦ Must be a satisfying read.

♦ Beyond the 'aww' factor.

♦ Uplifting/inspiring/stirring.

♦ Any strong theme.

♦ Emotional content.

Your inspiration
TV: *Life Begins, Cold Feet, William and Mary, Heart of Africa/ Springwatch* for nature themes. Heroic/courageous women: Odette, Marie Curie, Elizabeth Fry, Edith Cavell.

Long read: 2,800 words only: regular but not weekly
- Emotionally engaging.
- Light and shade.
- Strong continuous plot.
- Intrigue.
- Interwoven plot lines.
- Complex relationships.
- Recognisable people in recognisable situations.
- Escapist.
- Adventure.
- Balance of surprise vs expectations.

Your inspiration
Films: *Pay It Forward, Memoirs of a Geisha, Something's Gotta Give, It's A Wonderful Life, Dr Zhivago, Gone With The Wind.*
Novel: *Anne of Green Gables.*

Type of stories needed

Crime (medium read)
- From detective point of view.
- Victim fights back.
- Hustle/corporate con.

Your inspiration
TV: *New Tricks, Morse, Murder She Wrote, Whodunnit, Bergerac, Lovejoy, Cracker.* Grittier – *CSI Cold Case.*

Sting in the tale (1,500 words only)
- 'Clues' must not be misleading.
- Positive, pleasant outcome.
- Characters well rounded, need not always be likeable.
- Revenge (must not be vindictive).
- Misleading narrator.
- A nice surprise instead of a 'con'.

Your inspiration
Films: *Sixth Sense, The Others, The Village, The Usual Suspects.*
TV: *Hustle, Mobile, Fallen Angels, Tales of the Unexpected.*

Comedy/humour (short/medium/long read)
- Can be any length, as long as the theme warrants it.
- Concentrate on fun.
- Not cruel or at the expense of another character.
- Offbeat subjects.
- Unusual situations.
- Tongue-in-cheek can be fun.

Your inspiration
TV: *Two Fat Ladies, Hairy Bikers, Cheers, Friends, My Family* (sitcom), *Desperate Housewives, Boston Legal, The Good Life.*

Romance (short/medium/long read)
- Believable characters.
- Unusual themes/situations.
- Try not to be too predictable.
- Doesn't have to have a standard happy ending.
- Must still be hopeful.
- Inspiring.
- Light and shade work well.
- Try not to ring the changes with themes.

- Convincing emotions.
- Engaging dialogue.

Your inspiration
Films: *Truly Madly Deeply, Love Story, Benny and Joon, When Harry Met Sally, Notting Hill, Chocolat, Ghost*. Nicholas Sparks novels.

Nostalgic (short/medium/long read)
- From the 1950s up to present date.
- No First or Second World Wars.
- Can be set in a specific period.
- Flashback from present.
- Works well with music references of the period as a soundtrack for the story.
- Can be built around historical events.

Inspiration
TV: *Fame, The Liver Birds, The Good Life, Golden Girls, The Royal, The Darling Buds of May*, UKTV Gold! Film: *Grease*.

Historical (medium/long read)
- From the Second World War backwards (excluding the First World War).
- Themes must be generated from strictures of the time.
- Must be factually authentic and accurate.
- Need an accurate timeline.
- Less well-known eras/settings can work well.
- Must have positive message for present day.
- Can be set around historical event for figures.
- Atmosphere counts – accurate description adds to authenticity.

Your inspiration
TV/novels: *Cadfeal, I Claudius, Sharpe, Upstairs Downstairs.*
Films: *Shakespeare In Love, Gosford Park.*

Animal stories (short/medium/long read)
♦ Real relationship between human and animal.

Your inspiration
TV: *Spring Watch, Meerkat Manor, Heart of Africa*, any David Attenborough series. Novel: *Wolf Brother.*

Supernatural/sci fi/fantasy (short/medium/long read)
♦ Some suggestion of rational explanation.
♦ Not twee or laughable.
♦ Not gory or too shocking.

Your inspiration
Films: *Ghost, Sixth Sense.* TV: *Battlestar Galactica, Life on Mars, Dr Who, Babylon 5, X-Files.*

Emotional (medium/long read)
♦ Romance.
♦ Family issues.
♦ General relationships.
♦ Grief/divorce/loss.
♦ Life-changing events.

Your inspiration
TV: *Brother and Sisters, Casualty, Holby City, ER, Where The Heart Is.*

Best magazines guidelines

Every month, *Best* is sent hundreds of stories to consider for publication. To save your time and theirs, please don't send them yours unless it meets *all* of the following criteria. If you do send one, address it to the Fiction Editor, at *Best* magazine, 33 Broadwick Street, London, W1F 0DQ, and *print your name and address on the MS* (manuscript) (not just in the covering letter, which may become detached). Posted MSS must be sent with a stamped, self-addressed envelope for their return. Keep a copy, as *Best* cannot accept responsibility for the loss of unsolicited manuscripts. You can submit your story by e-mail, to *bestfiction@natmags.co.uk* – but they will need your postal address, so you can assign rights and they can pay you, if they decide to buy your story, so do include it.

- Your story must be original and not under consideration elsewhere.

- It should be no less than 900 and no more than 1,200 words long, and typewritten. Please do not send a disk or tape – these will be returned unread – or fax your story. *Best* does not require a synopsis or outline first, or have time to read these. And they don't publish serials or poetry.

- Your plot must be strong and convincing, its situations modern, relevant and believable. *Best* are happy to have sex feature in a story, as long as it's not too explicit. Characters must be believable, too, and people with whom readers can identify. (Please familiarise yourself with the magazine.) In almost all stories we print, the main character is a woman.

- Your approach should be young, fresh and lively. *Best* loves humour and welcome original twists and angles. The outcome of your story must leave the reader feeling satisfied. *Best* does *not* want to read that it was all a dream! They also do not want stories about the lottery, dating agencies, fortune-tellers or murdering a spouse. They don't want mystery characters who turn out to be twin brothers or sisters, or first-person stories 'written' by dogs or cats!

◆ Don't be afraid to be different, to step outside a rigid story-telling format, to jump – in time, space, plot or pace – rather than spelling everything out, as this stretches the reader's imagination. A good story is original, and will interest, involve, intrigue, surprise.

◆ *Best* works a minimum of two months in advance and, as MSS are not read immediately on arrival, seasonal stories need to be sent at least three and ideally four months ahead. Please note that MS turnaround time can be two to three months, and occasionally longer.

The People's Friend guidelines

Before you start ... *please study the market*. This is vitally important, because the 'Friend' has a very distinctive, individual approach to both fiction and features.

First, a bit about the most important people – the readers. Without them there would be no magazine!

They range in age from about thirty to well over eighty. They like being entertained – and dislike being depressed. They like realistic material, but not so realistic – with sex, violence, drugs, drink, etc

– that they are frightened or saddened. They still believe in the sanctity of marriage and the importance of the family. Our readers like people – ordinary people, with problems they can sympathise with, and in situations they can relate to. They're optimistic – they like to see something good coming out of a situation, or the redeeming side of a character. They're practical women – and men – with ordinary interests and hobbies. They're always willing to give a neighbour a helping hand and enjoy being with a group of friends.

Yes – they are traditionalist. And proud of it! So they like to see their values reflected in their 'Friend'. Many say that's exactly how they regard the magazine – as a friend.

So please, read *The People's Friend* for several weeks. Then, try to work out how the authors have achieved what the publisher wants.

But don't just write a carbon copy of something already published. Try to be original.

Complete stories
These vary in length – between 1,000 and 4,000 words usually. Deeper, more emotional, stories tend to need more space than lighter ones. *The Friend* also accepts short, short stories, from 500 to 1,000 words, for occasional complete-on-a-page fiction.

Friend readers like reading about people of any age. Don't fall into the trap of thinking they only use stories about grans and grandads, widows and widowers. Stories with older characters are, obviously, important but their readers also enjoy those with up-to-date, young, romantic themes. There's always a place for the light-hearted and humorous, too.

This isn't to say they avoid 'modern' themes like divorce or single parent families, but these must be treated sympathetically and tactfully.

They would rarely show divorce happening 'on stage' in a short story – or a serial. Separation that ends in reunion would be something their readers would approve wholeheartedly!

The Friend is always looking for good Christmas stories (as well as other seasonal material) but beware the well-worn themes! Again the message is – be original and try to reflect the real spirit of Christmas.

So what *don't* the readers enjoy?

Well, they've made it clear they don't want to read depressing, or bitter, stories. Or stories that shock or disgust or upset because of their graphic content – be it sex, violence or substance abuse.

And avoid the story with a 'twist in the tale' that misleads or cheats. Any twist has to be credible – and emotional.

Readers like to have a chuckle, or a lump in the throat, at the end of a story... or even both! But remember, they prefer to laugh with people rather than at them.

And they like to know how a character feels, as well as what he, or she, is doing. Write from the heart as well as the head – so that the emotion of the situation comes across strongly.

And the ending has to be satisfying.

The Friend rarely uses stories from the viewpoint of animals or inanimate objects. Historical short stories are difficult – it's not easy to be convincing in under 4,000 words. And anything with a supernatural theme tends to get the thumbs down from their very responsive readers.

In the author's byline *The Friend* frequently describes their stories as tender ... touching ... moving ... amusing ... charming ... All words with positive feelings behind them.

Your raw material is people. Readers want to identify with your characters, believe in them, their problems and the situations. If they can't get close to a character, or that character does or says something unconvincing, they'll lose interest. Your job is to keep the reader reading.

The Friend strongly suggests you try writing short stories before you attempt their other formats.

Serials
These are normally worked on from the early stages by the author and at least one member of staff. The storyline is carefully worked out by phone, letter, or by a face-to-face conference. Only when agreement is reached does the story proceed.

All *Friend* serials have a strong emotional situation as their central theme, usually family based. There can be other loosely connected storylines involving family members, relatives, friends... So it's quite in order to change viewpoints. It's even possible to do this in a first-person story – with a bit of ingenuity!

The Friend avoids subjects that are controversial, or which would be beyond the average reader's comprehension. They don't want to teach, or preach, or clamber on bandwagons. They don't want unusual, outrageous or offensive characters. This doesn't mean that characters have to be bland. Far from it. They must appeal to the reader's imagination and stir their emotions.

Your story can be set in the present day or it can be historical – without going too far back into the dim and distant past!

Writing a serial isn't like writing a novel. You have to enthral the reader in such a way that she – or he – is looking forward eagerly to next week's instalment. You don't have the luxury of writing long, beautifully crafted narrative or descriptive passages.

Serials run from ten to fifteen instalments on average, though *The Friend* will use shorter, or longer, stories from time to time.

The opening instalment is usually quite long – 6,000 or 7,000 words. You should aim to set the scene, introduce your characters and explain their problems.

Your opening page must catch and hold the reader's interest right away. Some problem, some crisis, should be coming to a head; some endeavour, some venture about to be undertaken...

Succeeding instalments are shorter, around 5,000 words.

Each instalment is made up of three or four chapters. (Get the idea of differentiating between a chapter and an instalment.)

Each chapter should deal with a particular aspect, or incident, or scene in the story, moving it forward at a good pace. Although there will naturally be some overlap, each chapter should be more or less complete, ending on a high point to encourage the reader to go on.

Don't jump around in short, quick, disjointed scenes. Give yourself a chance to develop your characters and their relationships.

Your final chapter to the instalment should have a more powerful curtain, so the reader is impatient to know what will happen next.

How your characters react – in their different ways – to the problems and situations you put them in, is what makes your *Friend* story. Your storyline – plot, if you like – is important, of course, but the reader will remember a good character long after she's forgotten other details.

Effective use of dialogue will not only build up your characters in the reader's mind, it can also provide background information.

Don't write long passages explaining what makes your character tick, or what's gone before. The reader should 'sense' their personality through what they say and how they react to challenging situations. Let the characters speak for themselves, so the reader can get involved and identify with them.

Study the popular soaps on TV. See how their writers use dialogue.

The People's Friend very rarely buys a complete serial in manuscript form. Don't even try a first instalment on your own!

Send them your idea, with perhaps just a few pages of the story, and give them a detailed synopsis of how the story develops... and they'll get back to you.

Fiction series

These might be considered a sort of hybrid, a cross between a short story and a serial. They are usually based on a strong, central character in an interesting situation. Each week's story is complete in itself and, in subsequent weeks, new characters and their problems are introduced.

But each story has a common setting and our central character is always there, playing a pivotal role.

Children's stories

These are traditional stories for children of nursery and primary age. Think of a bedtime story... nothing frightening, or disturbing, please. Humour is always welcome, and we'll also consider stories in verse. Length? Somewhere between 500 and 700 words.

Features

Friend readers always enjoy 'visiting' places up and down the country. These range from short, first-person experiences with a couple of pictures, to extensive photofeatures about a whole area, attraction or event. If you feel you want to try *photofeatures*, please contact *The Friend* first to discuss it. And, remember, there will be keen competition from established photographers and writers. *The Friend*'s standards are very high.

Filler features

These are usually about 1,000 words long. They're looking for bright, lively articles, full of human interest, on a broad range of topics. Animals... holidays... childhood... they should all have a strong personal involvement.

Poetry

Short lyric verse should rhyme and scan as naturally as possible. It must be easy to read so the meaning, or message, is clearly understood. Descriptive and 'mood' poetry is always popular.

Submitting a manuscript to The People's Friend

10 golden rules

- ◆ *The Friend* is always happy to consider unsolicited manuscripts, but once you've completed your story, try to read it objectively – they know it won't be easy, because you're so close to it and you've obviously put a lot of effort into it. But do try, and ask yourself – 'Is this really a *Friend* story?' And answer honestly, now! If the answer is a definite No, please don't send it in. But if you feel it's along the right lines, by all means let them see it. They are there to help and advise you.

- Your manuscripts should be typed – on one side of the paper only. Use double line spacing and leave a generous left-hand margin. *Always keep a copy.*

- You should also have a flysheet, showing the title and author's name (or pen-name if you prefer). Please make sure your own name and address also appear on the page.

- Number the pages of your story – or serial instalment.

- Staple or clip your manuscript once. And preferably use an A4 size envelope so that you don't have to fold the typescript over. Anything you can do to make your work easy to read will be much appreciated by their hard-working staff.

- Address your short stories to the Fiction Editor at the address below. Children's stories should be sent to the Children's Page Editor and poetry to the Poetry Editor and so on.

- Seasonal stories or articles should be submitted fully three months in advance.

- Remember to enclose a suitable stamped, addressed envelope. Or if you live abroad, send an International Reply Coupon.

- Please don't swamp *The Friend* with manuscripts! They very often find that a collection of stories all have the same basic flaw. So, if you've been enthusiastically writing, pick the best one – or two – to send in to test the water. It'll save your postage – and they'll let you know if they want to see more of your work.

- Be prepared to wait a few weeks for a reply. Our selection process can take some time.

Payment is on acceptance. You won't have to wait for publication.

Woman's Weekly guidelines

Woman's Weekly has always been well known for its short stories and serials, and fiction remains one of the most popular aspects of the magazine. Their readers talk about 'relaxing' with their short stories and serials, 'switching off' or 'taking a break' from the daily routine. However, *Woman's Weekly* are no longer looking for predictable boy-meets-girl romances or nostalgic looks at the past. Romance and nostalgia can be important parts of a story, but there should be other elements, too.

They want their stories to portray up-to-date characters in believable, modern situations. They welcome stories on a wide range of themes and moods, for instance, warm stories about children, teenagers and family problems of various kinds; love stories, funny stories and even stories with a crime or thriller element, so long as they are not violent, threatening or too incredible. In other words, fiction that grips the readers rather than sending them to sleep!

One of the main reasons for rejecting stories is that they can tell from the word go what their outcome will be. Unless there's an element of tension or uncertainty, readers won't bother to finish a story. And unless they can believe in the characters, they won't get involved in the first place. The best way to achieve this involvement is to be subtle in your writing. 'Show don't tell' is a useful maxim to bear in mind. And don't give away too much too soon. Tempt your reader on with more and more clues about a situation or character as the plot unfolds. Whatever you do, please don't tell *Woman's Weekly* the plot of your story in your covering letter! A surprise ending should be just that!

Taboos

Although they are far more flexible these days, there are still several 'don'ts' to bear in mind: whilst they welcome stories that reflect real life, they shouldn't contain explicit sex or violence. They will consider ghost stories but they mustn't be too frightening or horrific.

Short story lengths

Short stories in *Woman's Weekly* are usually either one page or two pages in length. For you, the writer, this means either 1,000 or 2,000 words long.

The bi-monthly *Fiction Special* accepts stories of between 1,000 and 5,000 words.

Serials

Serials should have all the compelling qualities of short stories plus strong characterisation and a well-researched background – and must also have riveting cliffhangers to keep the reader going back to the newsagent week after week. There should be a central 'hook' to hang the action on: an emotional or practical dilemma which the central character has to face. A strong subplot is essential. Historicals are just as welcome as contemporary serials.

Serials lengths

Serials can be between two and five parts. The opening instalment is 4,000 words, and each subsequent instalment is 3,500 words. You may submit the whole of your manuscript, or just the first part with a brief synopsis. *A synopsis alone cannot be considered*; *Woman's Weekly* needs to be able to assess your style, too.

General tips

Unfortunately *Woman's Weekly* cannot offer criticism, but if your short story or serial shows promise, they will contact you and suggest alterations.

It is most important that you read *Woman's Weekly* on a regular basis over several weeks before you submit your short story or serial. This is the only sure way to get the feel of our fiction.

Presentation

♦ *Woman's Weekly* read only typescripts – handwritten work cannot be considered.

♦ Preferred layout: double line spacing on one side of the paper only.

♦ Wide margins.

♦ Please number each page and make sure your name is at the top of each page.

♦ A stamped addressed envelope must be enclosed for the return of the manuscript if they are unable to use it. Remember, when sending in stories from abroad, please enclose an international reply coupon.

♦ If you would like an acknowledgement receipt of your manuscript, please enclose a stamped, addressed postcard.

♦ Please note that it can take up to sixteen weeks for manuscripts to be considered, and that *Woman's Weekly* are unable to enter into any correspondence by e-mail.

♦ Please send stories/serials to the following address: Gaynor Davies, Fiction Editor, *Woman's Weekly*, IPC Media, Blue Fin Building, 110 Southwark Street, London SE1 0SU.

Candis – short story guidelines

Debbie Attewell, Fiction Editor at *Candis*, says 'I personally read every short story submitted to *Candis*. Each month, three from the shortlist are sent out to that issue's reader panellists for their comments and I'll have the deciding vote if necessary. This ensures that the best story with the widest appeal is selected each month. The downside to this is that it can often be quite a long time between when you submit your fiction for consideration and when you hear whether you've been successful or not.' The following are *Candis*'s guidelines for submitting stories.

◆ Word count: 2000 +/– 10% (they will not read anything longer or vastly shorter than this).

◆ Who you're writing for: women aged 30–58 and their husbands/partners.

◆ What *Candis* are looking for: clever, keep 'em guessing story lines; twist in the tale/tales of the unexpected style writing. Stories of modern love, romance, friendship, family life. Short, tightly written whodunits. Warm likeable central characters.

◆ What Candis are *not* looking for: romantic stories with predictable endings; anything gory, detailed violence or graphic sexual descriptions.

◆ Short stories to be sent in the first instance by e-mail to: fiction@candis.co.uk.

◆ Fee: £500 payable on written acceptance.

Good luck!

(2)

Good Idea!

Where do you get your ideas from? I'm always being asked this question and my answer is always the same. Life.

All around you, are ideas. The trick is to notice them. Sometimes we can be so busy rushing through life that we fail to notice the little things. And as a writer, I firmly believe that it's the details which count. It's the man opposite you in the train who's been chattering on his mobile since you left Kings Cross and is still talking an hour later. Is he talking to his wife or is he flirting with his female boss? Why is he frowning? And what did he mean when he said that 'We'll need to sort that out by the end of the week'? It could, of course, be totally innocuous.

On the other hand, he might be up to no good. And it's up to you, as the writer, to decide. If you notice a situation or person who could be interesting, ask yourself the question 'What if?' What if they did something different? What if they weren't in the place they said they were going to? What if the tide came in unexpectedly? What if a big storm brewed up?

'What if' can be one of the best ways I know to think up ideas for a short story. Try it now. Make a list of situations which have caught your eye and ask yourself the 'What if' question. Then write down a list of answers.

Here are some situations which might trigger off some ideas for you:

- Parents' evening, next month.
- Battery runs out so the alarm clock doesn't go off.
- Delay at the traffic lights so you miss your train.
- Teaching your teenager how to drive.
- Signing up for an adult beginners swimming class.

Now ask yourself, 'What if?'

- What if the parents' evening was cancelled and no one told you?
- What if you overslept and as a result, you were still at home when someone unexpected called.
- What if you met an old friend on the later train.
- What if your teenager taught you something during his lesson?
- What if you were the teacher of the swimming class instead of a pupil?

See? You've already got a few ideas, haven't you? And that's just the beginning. We've already talked about the importance of buying a large, brightly-coloured Ideas Book as well as a smaller one for your handbag or pocket. Now write down these ideas and let them germinate in your mind. You might not have a full outline in your head – in fact, the chances are that you won't. But you may well have the seed of an idea.

Now you need time to let that idea grow. Keep it in your head as you go about your life and go back to it from time to time. Often, the idea will come back to you without any prompting. And almost miraculously, you'll begin to realise what you could do with it. The male character could get another job and that will lead him to the heroine. A child might find something that's hidden under the floorboards. The grandmother in your original idea might refuse to move out of her house. Anything can happen, providing you allow your imagination to run free.

WHAT ARE YOU GOOD AT?

I also believe that writers write best about what they know. Clearly, this isn't always the truth since we hope that crime writers won't necessarily have committed a crime! But they will have done their research. They will probably have interviewed someone who has broken the law and also someone who helps to keep the law.

I'll be talking about research in Chapter 18 on using the internet but in the meantime, it's useful to think about what you are good at. This is usually the point when some of my students claim they're not good at anything. 'I don't work any more,' said one of my class the other day. 'I just look after the children.'

Just? Not only is this one of the most difficult (as well as rewarding) jobs in the world but it's also a fertile ground for fiction ideas. There's nothing like children for making you see things differently and for introducing you to other adults and children whom you might not come across in life. And this is what the stuff of fiction is made of.

I would find it very difficult to write my novels and short stories without having had three children. Let me give you an example. The other day, I was going through my linen bin, sorting out clothes for a wash. Now two of my children only live at home for part of the time because they're older, so usually there isn't a great deal left in my linen bin. But this week, they were all present so my linen bin was teeming. As I went through each item, deciding which wash it needed to go through, I began noticing certain clues on the garments which told me what the children had been up to. There was a grass stain on my daughter's skirt. A note screwed up in my son's jean pockets. And a girl's item of clothing in one of my other son's pockets!

That got me thinking. I didn't immediately form a story in my head but the clothes idea germinated over the next few days. And I then wrote a story called 'The Laundry Basket' in which the heroine learns something about her family – as well as herself – by going through each item of clothing. You'll find the story at the end of this chapter.

That's what I mean by using your specialisation. But there are others too. If you are a doctor, you will know about all kinds of areas which the rest of us won't. If you work on the check-out till at the supermarket, you'll have had lots of opportunities to people-watch. How did that woman react when she couldn't find her purse to pay the bill? Why did that man have 30 tins of sardines? Was that couple at the end of the queue, really a husband and wife or a mother and son?

Perhaps you've got a friend who has an interesting job. Ask him or her to tell you about it. Providing people aren't going to be named in the novel, they are happy to tell you lots of things 'off the record', especially if it's going to be fictionalised.

WORD OF MOUTH

Listening to other people's stories will also give you plenty of ideas for short stories. So keep your eyes and ears open, wherever you are. Some years ago, I was on a bus when I overheard two girls talking. Their conversation went like this:

> *'Hasn't he got the most amazing legs you've ever seen.'*
>
> *'And have you seen his eyes? They look right into you.'*
>
> *'I can't wait to see him again.'*

By this time, the entire bus was riveted. And then the first girl said:

> *'With my luck, they'll give me the other horse to ride next time.'*

It's a great story isn't it – and one which you could play around with before that final twist in the tale. (See Chapter 9.)

Other people's stories can be a fantastic source of ideas. One of the exercises I do with my weekly class of students is to divide them into pairs. Each one then has to tell the other about something memorable that's happened to them or someone they know in the past year. If they can't think of anything, their partner has to ask them probing questions such as 'When were you last scared?' or 'What was the most valuable thing you've ever lost?'

This usually prompts some response. We then have a class discussion in which the person who has heard the story, has to tell the rest of the class about their partner's story and we then see if it might form the seed for a short story or novel. I do it this way because a good writer needs to listen besides talking and writing. I've heard some incredible stories this way.

NEWSPAPERS, MAGAZINES AND THE NET

This is a vital source of ideas. Factual features can give you all kinds of ideas for fiction. Take the following articles which I cut out this week for my class. There was a piece on mothers who choose to give birth at home. This might give you an idea for a story about a woman who went into labour in an unusual place. It doesn't have to stick to the original; but the piece might trigger off ideas to expand it.

Then there was a story about a woman who had started a business specialising in the colour purple. Everything she sold was purple. What a good way of making your character stand out if they will only wear one colour.

Don't forget the problem page. This is a fantastic fodder ground for stories. Take the woman who has just seen her best friend's husband kissing another woman in the car park. Should she tell her friend or let sleeping dogs lie? I can definitely feel a short story coming on with that one; preferably one with a twist at the end that explains the husband is innocent.

The internet is a good source as well, although there's the danger here that you might get so involved in looking at possible ideas, that you don't get down to the actual business of writing. Still, ignore it at your peril. Google in 'Strange things' and see what you come up with. Or Google 'coincidences' and try that out for size.

Look up unusual sites and see if they inspire you. Perhaps you could write a short story about someone who is inspired to change their life as a result of browsing the web. The possibilities are endless.

USING PICTURES

Use pictures and photographs to think up stories. Remember that picture you took of the family having a meal in the Spanish hotel last year? Who is the man sitting at the table next to you? And why is he looking at your wife like that? It's probably totally innocent but once you start writing, it could be a different story.

Cut out pictures from magazines and newspaper supplements. Ask yourself what the person in the picture has just been doing and what he or she is about to do. What job are they putting off? Do they have a mother who is waiting to hear from them? Are they excited about something or are they dreading the next day? Hopefully, this might start triggering off ideas.

Keep these pictures in a folder because in Chapter 3 on characterisation, I want you to do something else with these pictures!

TELEVISION AND RADIO

Listen to the radio and television. Take time out and call it research. All kinds of programmes can trigger off ideas. That programme on other people's houses might make you think of a short story about an estate agent who, unknown to his buyers, is actually selling his own home.

Keep the radio on when you're driving or take it into the bathroom. Listen to programmes you might not normally listen to. I did that the other night and caught a programme about real-life confessions. It was about a woman who had lied on her CV at work and was actually older than she said she was. She was now scared she was going to be caught out. That gave me the idea for a short story about someone's CV and what it told us about the real person behind the facts (and fiction).

RESEARCHING YOUR IDEA

You don't always need to do research for your short story. But it can help. If you want to know what an estate agent really does all day or what a policeman does in his lunch break, there's no substitute for talking to someone.

Similarly, use the internet and also the local library to look up something. You might find you get more ideas on the way.

USING YOUR TRAVEL EXPERIENCE

Going on holiday when all you want to do is write? Use your travel experience to widen your knowledge and write about it. I wrote a short story about a woman who was given the wrong suitcase by mistake at the airport. Through it, she learned a lot about the man who really owned it which was good preparation for when she met him.

◆ Write down a list of unusual things which have happened to you or other people.

◆ What kind of stories could you make from them?

—— THE LAUNDRY BASKET ——
(this first appeared in *Woman's Weekly*)

ONE PAIR OF BOXERS. Medium size. Grey.
Well they should be white but somehow over time, they've become a distinct grey. I don't know how these washing ads do it. Well I do – they must put something extra in it – but whatever it is, it's not in my wash. Not that Nick will notice. 16 year old boys don't. It's only their mothers. I would get him some new ones but I'm not entirely sure now if he's grown into a Large. It's not the kind of thing that teenage boys discuss easily with their mothers. 'Are your boxers too tight?' isn't exactly a tactful question when your son's just brought a new girlfriend home and is watching a video on the sofa downstairs. I'll just have to remember to ask him later. Meanwhile, I'll carry on sorting.

ONE SKIMPY T-SHIRT. So-called one-size. Pink.
Must make sure this doesn't go into the white wash. Must also remember to put it on 30 degrees and not 60 like last time. Anna wasn't very pleased about that and I can see why. 'It's difficult when there are five people in the house who all need their washing done,' I explained. She gave me the kind of look that only 15 year old daughters can. 'Mum, it says Cold Wash Only. You can't get clearer than that.' True. Some items in my laundry basket are positively secretive like this...

CHARITY-BUY SUMMER DRESS.
Well, it seemed like a good idea at the time. Just feel it. Nice isn't it? Possibly silk or maybe an imitation. And a lovely cornflower-blue colour that matches my eyes, apparently. The only trouble is that there isn't a washing-instructions label inside. Still, I haven't been doing the washing for all these years for nothing. I

know that silk needs to go on the Silk setting. It's a pity that my new washing machine doesn't seem to have one of these. The old one did. But this one seems to lump it all together under 'Special Care'. Well, that will do. Won't it?

PALE BLUE JEANS.
Extra large. Perfect for casual weekends. Owned by the man who says I have cornflower blue eyes. Easy. 40 degree wash. Never goes wrong because it comes from a nationally-revered chain store with reliable washing instructions. So I can put that one straight into the pale colour pile.

BLACK THONG PANTS.
Well, I haven't seen these before! Anna must have bought these recently or else ... no I don't even want to think about the other possibility although it has been known for Nick's pockets to contain all sorts of things that a mother should never have to see. Just for fun, I hold them against me and glance in the bathroom mirror. Does my derriere look big in this? Don't even answer that question. Good heavens. The price sticker is still inside. How on earth can a pair of thongs – which look all wrong on me – cost so much? They actually cost three times as much as...

KIM'S NEW DESIGNER JEANS.
I don't believe in designer jeans for 13-year-olds either. But we found these at a discount store that her friends all go to and I have to say that I was pleasantly surprised at the price tag. What I'd like to know, however, is just what she's been doing to them since we bought them last week. They've got self-inflicted cuts slashed across the knees and holes – which I swear weren't there at the time of purchase or I wouldn't have got them. 'It's the fashion,' said Anna when she poked her head round the door to see if her own jeans were ready yet (just ten more minutes in the tumble drier). 'All the kids have ripped jeans nowadays. The more air, the more flair.' No surprises for guessing that Anna wants to study fashion. Which brings me onto...

NICK'S DESIGNER JEANS.
Pity that I can't persuade him to go to discount stores any more. These may not

have holes but in my view, the quality doesn't justify the price. I know because I helped pay for them. Still, there are advantages in doing the washing for your teens. You get to know quite a lot about their lives when they're careless enough not to empty their pockets. I didn't know that he went to the çinema last Thursday night. He told me he'd gone to the library but here are two cinema stubs to prove it. And what's this in the other pocket? A school detention slip. Not another! We'll have to have words about that and then I'll have to confess I found it in his jeans. I'm not a nosy mother – please don't think that. It's just that I like to keep track of my kids. When they don't tell you much about their lives, their pockets are the only things you have to go by.

ANNA'S CREAM SKIRT.
I was quite pleased when she said she wanted a skirt. Girls nowadays don't seem to wear them. But when she brought this one home, I thought it was a scarf. Seriously. It only just covers the vital bits. And it's got a big green stain on the rear which means she's been sitting on the grass again with her friends talking about their mothers. Either that or . . . no. I don't even want to think why else she might have been sitting on the grass. Well, maybe I do. Perhaps I'll have a little chat with her later on as well as Nick. Meanwhile, how am I going to get the stain out?

ODD ASSORTMENT OF SOCKS.
Including three greens, one brown and a grey singleton. I think there was one grey one left over from the last wash so if I can find it, I might make a pair. Sometimes doing the laundry seems more like Pelmanism. You just have to remember where you put the matching one.

PAIR OF TIGHTS.
Which have become inexplicably bound up with my husband's pyjama bottoms. I giggle, thinking about last night. And then it happens. 'Help!' I call out. 'Help!'

TWO WEEKS LATER.
I need two laundry baskets now. And they're both overflowing, mainly with pink items. Until nine months ago, I thought I was past all that but life's full of

surprises, isn't it? Maybe that's why I was sorting out the laundry basket until the last minute. They say it's the nesting instinct before you go into labour. Unfortunately, that meant the kids had to do the washing when I was away. The results are as follows:

One pair of pink boxers. One pink skirt. (Well, at least it hides the grass stain.) One pair of my husband's blue jeans, now extra small. Several clothing items with bits of school notes attached, now unreadable. And a cornflower-blue summer dress. Doll size.

Still, as Anna says, it's a great excuse to go shopping. All six of us.

3

Nice to Meet You!

HOW TO WRITE CONVINCING CHARACTERS FOR SHORT STORIES

Characters in short stories are both different from and similar to characters in a novel. They're different because you have far less space, time and opportunity to persuade the reader that the character you are painting on the page could be a real person. Therefore you have to get in there fast.

You don't have the luxury of time to build up a picture over several chapters. Instead, you need to do a thumbnail sketch of a character almost immediately, in order to draw the reader in. You must find a way of using a few words to show how a character thinks, talks, behaves and interacts with other characters.

You also need to show that each paper character has a 'voice'; something which makes him or her stand out from the others. Otherwise, the reader's going to wonder why you need that character at all.

There's also less time to show how your character is changing – if indeed he or she is going to change. In a novel, part of the plot usually hinges around a problem that the character (or characters) has to solve or come to terms with. As part of this, at least one character has to go through a learning curve and make some big changes. Often these changes involve his views on the world or even his or her lifestyle. If you've got 800 words or even 2,000 words, the scope for doing this is clearly limited.

So how do we build characterisation?

This is where the similarities with a character in a novel come in. When I teach my classes, I stress that a convincing character has to have certain mannerisms or quirks or eccentricities or a way of behaving that makes him or her stand out from other people.

The best way to pinpoint these mannerisms is to think of people whom you know in real life who stand out in your mind. You might not necessarily like them, but they do things that you can't quite get out of your head.

I'd like you now to make a list of these people. To get you started, I'll give you some ideas of my own, taken from both my own experience and those of students in my classes who have given permission for this.

- A woman who is always checking her reflection every time she passes a mirror.

- Someone who always has the television on when you visit.

- A character who wears a lot of black (or any other single colour).

- Someone who ends their sentence in a question mark.

- A character who keeps fidgeting and just can't stay still.

- Someone who's always sniffing and doesn't blow their nose.

- A character who's always on the scrounge, e.g. a neighbour who's constantly running out of tea or coffee, etc.

◆ Someone who speaks in deep voice or a high, squeaky voice. This works particularly well when the voice doesn't seem to fit the character, such as an elderly woman sounding like a little girl.

◆ A person who stutters.

◆ A character who has poor posture and is always slouching.

◆ Someone who holds himself very straight like a member of the military.

◆ A character who walks with a limp or a stick.

◆ Someone who's always talking about money.

◆ A character who's often telling jokes.

◆ Someone who's always pessimistic . . . or optimistic.

Now I'd like you to make your own list. After that, read through it carefully. Do any of them jump out at you? It's important to write about characters you feel passionate about. After all, if you don't convince the reader, you won't convince yourself either.

The next step is to see which of these characters you could portray reasonably quickly in a short story.

'Trademark' dialogue

Someone who always speaks in a certain way, for example, can be identified quite soon through their dialogue. Supposing you had a character who always said 'know what I mean?' at the end of every sentence. This is what I call a 'trademark phrase': a figure of speech which someone uses regularly.

I'll explain more about this in Chapter 6 on dialogue but, in the meantime, it serves as a good example for establishing character fast. If your man or woman says 'know what I mean?' every time he or she speaks, we have an idea of the kind of person they might be.

Getting more complex

Now let's add the layers. Let's pretend they're a worrier as well. (I'm a born worrier so this is easy!) We could then introduce a character with the following paragraph.

> *'I thought something had happened to you,' said John as soon as his sister got off the bus half an hour later than planned. 'We're going to be late now. Know what I mean?'*

Already, we can tell this man is fretting about something. And because the 'Know what I mean?' comes rather awkwardly at the end of the line, it shows us that he's the kind of person who isn't very good at articulating himself.

Let's take another example. Perhaps his sister Mary is exactly the opposite.

> *'You worry too much,' said Mary giving him a warm cuddle. 'I've told you before; it will be all right in the end. You'll see.'*

In just two lines, we can see that Mary is a kindly sort of woman. She's also reassuring. And she's the sort of person who firmly believes that everything will turn out fine ultimately. The words 'You'll see' is another trademark phrase that people say again and again. We can use it to herald Mary's presence.

Now let's add yet another layer. Supposing Mary doesn't go anywhere without taking her dog. It might be a large, brown, smelly Labrador who loves people and is always clamouring for attention. I'm going to call him Mungo because that's the name of my dog in my new novel *The Supper Club*.

(By the way, I always have a dog in each one of my books because I think they help define people and bring out their characters. There's always going to be someone who doesn't like a dog and that can create fantastic friction in my cast. I also have an elderly Labrador of my own so know a bit about them.)

Now let's see Mary's dog getting off the bus with her to greet Mary's brother.

> *'Down, Mungo, down.' Mary pulled her large brown Labrador away from John. 'I'm so sorry. Oh dear, his paws are rather muddy, aren't they? Don't worry. We can clean you up before the interview.'*

Immediately, Mungo has helped us reinforce the picture of Mary. She's the kind of person who loves dogs and is perhaps used to mess. Again, she's not too worried about John's dirty trousers. And even better, Mungo has moved us on to the next stage of the plot. Suddenly, we find out that John has an interview.

Of course, you don't have to have dogs as a 'prop' for your character. Many of my fictional friends have children, ranging from tantrumming toddlers to totally impossible teens. I call these the 'satellite props' because although they exist in their own right as characters, they also show us something about the main ones.

And again, they can be very useful in short stories for drawing that thumbnail sketch fast.

MOVING THE CHARACTER ON

How else can we establish a character fast in the limited space we have for a short story? As I will show you in Chapter 4 on plot and pace, we can give them a problem which has to be sorted out fast.

There isn't the luxury in 800 words or even 1,800 to create a long lead-up to this problem. We need to get in there fast; we have to present it quite soon so the character can get his or her teeth into it.

Creating sympathy

On the other hand, we also need to know the character a bit before they tackle the problem. Otherwise, we won't have enough sympathy for him or her. When I explain this to my weekly classes, I ask them to imagine passing a road accident and seeing someone on a stretcher being carried into an ambulance. Most of us would feel a pang of worry and sympathy for that person and his or her family.

But if we knew that person and he wasn't a stranger, we would be distraught, wouldn't we? Our hearts would be pounding; we might feel sick; and I bet there'd be a feeling of disbelief which is an emotion we often feel when something unexpected happens.

It's a bit like that when something happens to a character we don't know very well. You know you ought to feel compassion and perhaps shock if something terrible happens to them. But if the writer hasn't allowed enough time or inserted adequate detail to help us get to know them, we won't fully engage in their predicament.

But how do we do this in a short space of time – and how quickly can we set about it? My own feeling on this is that you should be able to draw a character within three or four paragraphs. After that, you could put in the predicament so that we are willing the character to 'win'. In other words, solve the problem.

Take this example which comes from a short story I wrote for *Woman's Weekly*.

Holiday Baggage

That was it, I told myself as I checked in my case in at the airport. No more blind dates! Not even one teeny, weeny one. This holiday was going to be a fresh start. If my sister Sharon wanted me to make up a foursome on the beach, that was too bad. All I wanted was some sun and time to myself; something I badly needed after the past year.

'Come on, Jenny,' said Sharon impatiently, who'd checked in before me. 'We've got two whole hours of sightseeing before we board the plane. What are you waiting for?'

Sightseeing, in my sister's book, was spotting any man over 5'11" without a wedding ring on his left hand.

I shook my head firmly. 'Sorry Sharon, but we've been through this one before. I'm not here to find a boyfriend. I'm here to find me.'

Sharon eyed me quizzically. 'You've been reading too many self-help books. Find yourself, indeed! You're standing right here in Departures, just in front of a gorgeous guy who is giving you the once-over even though you're blindly ignoring him. Too late, he's gone.'

See what I mean? Sharon was incorrigible and I was beginning to wonder why I'd agreed to go on holiday with her in the first place. As sisters, we were like chalk and cheese. She was the go-getter and I was . . . well I'm not sure. Sometimes I'm daring enough to do things that even Sharon wouldn't do and sometimes, I just want to wrap myself up in a cocoon and be on my own.

Maybe that's why Peter had left. 'I don't understand you,' he'd said on more than one occasion. Well, I didn't understand him, either. Or, to be precise, I didn't understand how he could be seeing someone else and going out with me at the same time.

Hopefully, in the above example, we've got an idea about our heroine Jenny's character. She's quite firm-minded (determined not to look for a boyfriend on holiday). She's had a tough year and needs a break. Oh yes, and she has a slightly pushy sister. (More of whom, later.)

You might recognise some of these characteristics in yourself. A lot of people will have been through tough times in the past, so we are probably going to feel quite sympathetic about that. We like the fact that she's firm about not looking for a boyfriend because we're already beginning to hope that she does find one – or else something else to make her happy. Those of us with sisters (such rich fodder for fiction!) will identify with our heroine dealing with Sharon. And even if we don't have sisters, we probably have well-meaning relatives or friends who can be a bit of a pain in the neck.

All right. So we've set up the character. Now what's the problem? Here we are, at the luggage carousel in Spain, after the flight. You know the feeling, don't you? You're standing there, hoping your suitcase hasn't been lost even though everyone else around you seems to have theirs.

I heaved my navy blue suitcase off the belt. 'You might be. But I'm here to ...'

'Read all those boring books you've got inside that thing,' finished my sister.

Exactly. I couldn't wait to unpack my new Sebastian Faulkes and lie down with him on a sunbed. Except that by the time we got to our room, I discovered Sebastian wasn't there.

'I don't believe it,' I cried, staring into my suitcase on the hotel bed. 'I've got the wrong bag.'

'You can't have,' said Sharon, opening hers. 'Mine's all right. And we put them on at the same time.'

I pulled out a pair of blue and red swimming trunks with a 40-inch waist label.

'Suits you,' giggled Sharon. 'They'll get you noticed all right.'

By this time, I was going all hot and cold, trying to remember what I'd packed and what might now have gone for ever. At least six expensive thick paperbacks which I'd been dying to read. A nearly-new bottle of Chanel No 5 which mum had given me for my birthday. A travelling alarm clock. A brand-new bikini which had taken several hours to find (am I the only woman whose bottom has very little in common with her top?). And a pair of flat sandals because I meant it about finding myself. I intended to explore the area which would be difficult in the more elegant shoes I had travelled in.

Instead, I had the following items in front of me. The swimming trunks (enough said). A travelling clock. Six thick blokey action-type books, including two by Robert Harris, whom I'd never read. A blank sketchpad. A rather nice cable green jersey. A pair of trainers size 11. Several T-shirts and shorts, none of which were folded particularly neatly. One of those cheap disposable cameras. A tennis racquet. And a magnetic draughts set.

Interesting. We now have a character we've never actually met. Except that we do know a bit about him from his possessions. Swimming trunks which means he's an outdoor type: something that's compounded by the tennis racquet. A sketchpad which suggests means he might be an artist. A disposable camera which might mean he isn't very technical or else he'd have a digital. And a draughts set (nerd or what?).

I hope you'll want to read on. (If you do, the entire story is at the end of this chapter.) But I think you'll agree that in a few paragraphs, we already have quite a good sense of three characters as well as understanding what the problem is. And if any of you have been stuck on holiday without your luggage or with someone else's by mistake, you'll sympathise with our heroine's dilemma. Even if you haven't, you can still imagine it's the type of problem which might happen so easily to you, that you can visualise it quite clearly.

HOW MANY IS TOO MUCH?

In the above example, there are three main characters as well as a fourth surprise one towards the end. There is also a fleeting reference to our heroine's ex-boyfriend although he doesn't figure largely as a character.

This, in fact, is the beauty of short stories. You can refer to someone else and, providing you provide a few details about him or her, we don't need to see them fully. We know by now that Peter is unreliable. And that's enough for the time being.

But that still leaves us with the question of how many characters can tip the boat? I'm sure you've all read novels where there were so many people that you had to keep flicking back and forwards to check who was who.

Well you just can't do that in a short story. For a start, if your cast is too big, the reader fails to bond with the small number that the author needs them to bond with. After all, there just isn't enough space to get to know everyone.

It's rather like someone who has a crowd of 'intimate' friends. If a friend is really a good one, you need a lot of time with him or her.

Retaining the reader's interest

The other interesting – and scary – point about short stories is that if the reader gets confused or bored or simply fed up, she or he will merely turn over the page. There isn't the investment they might have put in a novel. You know what it's like. If you're half way through a novel, you feel you ought to finish it. It almost feels like giving up if you don't. But there isn't that obligation with a short magazine story because it is, after all, just for fun. Or at least, it should be.

This puts huge pressure on you, as the writer, to produce a story that the reader is going to carry on reading. And if you have too many characters or a boring plot and unbelievable dialogue, they won't.

The good news is that if you have a containable cast of characters who create a wonderful pot-pourri of fun, excitement, tension and story, you'll have them hooked.

Limiting the number of characters

I personally believe that the writer is wise to limit the number of characters to three or – at the most – four in a story. You also need to make sure that every character has his or her own voice in order to make them stand out from the others.

You can do this through the methods I've described at the beginning of the chapter by creating mannerisms and so on. You can also do it through dialogue (see Chapter 6).

And you can do it through showing the interaction between characters themselves. We've already seen some of the tension between our heroine and her sister Sharon. They're very different, aren't they? And that's one of the forces that drives the characters and plot forward.

Take the following example:

> *'Only trying to help,' said Sharon pretending to be hurt.*
>
> *I gave her a sisterly squeeze.*
>
> *'I don't need to worry, you know,' she pointed out. 'I've got years ahead to find someone. But people like you need a helping hand. Hey, look at that one. With his mates around him. He's looking at us too ... Jenny, where are you going?'*

Jenny's doing a runner. And with a sister like that, I don't blame her.

DO WE REALLY LIKE THE CHARACTER?

It's essential that, in both novels and short stories, we love our characters. Of course they've got faults. But we need to like them and understand that, just like us, they're not perfect.

Jenny, in our story, might seem rather stubborn but we know enough about her to see why. She's been hurt in the past and she's scared of being hurt again.

We also like her sister Sharon, despite ourselves. Sharon is only trying her best for her sister. She just does it in her own way.

Adding an 'interesting' character

As I've already said, we don't warm to Peter but that's fine. After all, if all our characters were likeable, there might not be much of a plot. We need to have someone who is difficult and who can then make the others act or not act in a way that adds to the story.

And that's where the baddy comes in. In a novel, we have the luxury of time to build up a picture of a baddy. But not in a short story. So how do we do it? As we've seen with Peter, you don't even need to introduce the baddy in person. You can merely use a few well-chosen words and phrases to show that someone isn't very nice. (See my 'Holiday Baggage' story on pages 54–61.)

In some stories, however, it's essential to see the baddy in action. But we need to make sure that, in our limited number of words, we don't overdo him or her – otherwise the baddy could take over.

We therefore need the baddy to have a fairly brief time on stage, leaving the other characters time to sort out what to do. Otherwise, we are left with that rather nasty taste in our mouth when really our aim, as a short-story writer, is to create a good taste.

DO WE REALLY WANT THEM?

You've probably heard of the phrase 'Kill off your darlings'. I don't like clichés but I have to admit that this is a fairly accurate description of what you have to do when working out which characters you should get rid of.

But why get rid of any? And who should you kill off, if you have to? I see this rather like a redundancy situation. Imagine you're the boss of a fairly small firm. Every now and then, you have to make staff appraisals. This means looking at each member of your workforce and seeing what they contribute – and if you really need them.

EXERCISE

I'd like you to do this with every one of your characters. (This also applies to novels too.) Make a list of the characters and next to their name, write down what their role is and why you need them. Then imagine you are taking them out of your story. What would you lose if you did that? If the answer is very little, consider handing them their P45.

It might be that your characters could job-share instead. In other words, you could merge them into one so they fulfil both functions and also make your cast of characters tidier and more manageable.

I originally had Peter featuring more prominently in my story 'Holiday Baggage' but decided this complicated matters. He also seemed more interesting at a distance.

WHAT'S IN A NAME?

I was once advised by a fiction editor never to have characters' names beginning with the same letter – even if they were of different sexes. So don't, for instance, have an Alan and an Aileen. Although you might think the fact that one is a man and one is a woman is enough, it could still confuse the reader if they're reading a short story quickly.

Just as important, avoid similarly-sounding names like George and Julia. You need to have a crisper difference in order to help that character establish his or her voice.

Resources for names

If you're stuck for names, look through baby name books and also the newspapers (births, deaths and marriages normally have some good ideas). Be careful not to have a name which people will have problems pronouncing or which represents the kind of person they might not naturally identify with. For example, an upper class name like Clarissa might alienate your reader if she is the main character whom you are asking people to root for.

On the other hand, it could help to create exactly the kind of person you want to portray. For instance, someone who gets up everyone else's nose.

—— Holiday Baggage ——
by Sophie King
(originally printed in *Woman's Weekly*)

That was it, I told myself as I checked in my case in at the airport. No more blind dates! Not even one teeny, weeny one. This holiday was going to be a fresh start. If my sister Sharon wanted me to make up a foursome on the beach, that was too bad. All I wanted was some sun and time to myself; something I badly needed after the past year.

'Come on, Jenny,' said Sharon impatiently, who'd checked in before me. 'We've got two whole hours of sightseeing before we board the plane. What are you waiting for?'

Sightseeing, in my sister's book, was spotting any man over 5'11", without a wedding ring on his left hand.

I shook my head firmly. 'Sorry Sharon, but we've been through this one before. I'm not here to find a boyfriend. I'm here to find me.'

Sharon eyed me quizzically. 'You've been reading too many self-help books. Find yourself, indeed! You're standing right here in Departures, just in front of a gorgeous guy who is giving you the once-over even though you're blindly ignoring him. Too late, he's gone.'

See what I mean? Sharon was incorrigible and I was beginning to wonder why I'd agreed to go on holiday with her in the first place. As sisters, we were like chalk and cheese. She was the go-getter and I was . . . well I'm not sure. Sometimes I'm daring enough to do things that even Sharon wouldn't do and sometimes, I just want to wrap myself up in a cocoon and be on my own.

Maybe that's why Peter had left. 'I don't understand you,' he'd said on more than one occasion. Well, I didn't understand him, either. Or, to be precise, I didn't understand how he could be seeing someone else and going out with me at the same time.

My friends all rallied round with sympathy hugs and cries of 'He wasn't good enough for you'. But it was Sharon who told me that at my age, I'd better pull myself together and find someone else. And that's how the blind dates started.

Don't ask me why I agreed but even though Sharon is younger than me by a good five years, she's always been streets ahead in that department. 'I've got the perfect man,' she announced one day over the phone. 'He's tall, single and not as boring as Peter was. He wants to meet you too. I said you were free after work tonight.'

Well I didn't want to offend the poor chap, especially as he shared Sharon's office and might, as she told me firmly, make life very difficult for her if I turned him down. But the date was a complete disaster. I mean, would you go out with a man who bred hamsters for a hobby and still lived with his mother at

35? I might have tried a bit harder if he hadn't proceeded to tell me, all through dinner, about the breeding habits of hamsters. Believe me, you don't want to know.

Sharon's next blind date wasn't much better. I'm a simple girl at heart; not fussy, you understand. I enjoy going out to the cinema and parties but I also like to curl up in a chair with a good book and glass of wine. Dennis, whose sister-in-law's friend worked out with Sharon at the gym (not my favourite place) didn't have time to read and preferred to watch the telly instead of forking out good money at the cinema when the film would be available on video in a few months' time.

In fact, that's why Sharon and I were here at the airport, right now. We were walking to the cinema when we happened to pass the travel agent. And there, slap-bang in the window, was such a good last-minute deal to Menorca that you'd have to have been as boring as Peter (Sharon's words) to have ignored it.

Somehow, I managed to wangle a week off from my boss and Sharon (who was very good at wangling all sorts of things with hers) went ahead and booked before I could change my mind. 'One rule,' I said firmly. 'This is not a man-hunting exercise. This is a break away from that sort of thing. If you find someone, fine. But don't ask him to bring a mate along.'

'Fair enough,' said Sharon airily but by the time we landed at Menorca, I began to think I should have got her to sign a pre-holiday deal. 'Oooh, look at him,' she said, pointing to a tall dark man in shorts, at the front of the passport queue. 'He's gorgeous! And he's on his own too. No he's not. Damn. Where did she come from?'

'The loo actually,' I pointed out. 'Isn't a man allowed to stand on his own for two seconds before you get your telescopic vision into him?'

'Only trying to help,' said Sharon pretending to be hurt. I gave her a sisterly squeeze. 'I don't need to worry, you know,' she pointed out. 'I've got years ahead to find someone. But people like you need a helping hand. Hey, look at that one. With his mates around him. He's looking at us too ... Jenny, where are you going?'

I was almost dragging her by the hand towards the luggage carousel. 'To get our cases and stop you making a fool of yourself. Honestly, he could hear you.'

'So what? He'll know we're free too.'

I heaved my navy blue suitcase off the belt. 'You might be. But I'm here to ...'

'Read all those boring books you've got inside that thing,' finished my sister.

Exactly. I couldn't wait to unpack my new Sebastian Faulkes and lie down with him on a sunbed. Except that by the time we got to our room, I discovered Sebastian wasn't there.

'I don't believe it,' I cried, staring into my suitcase on the hotel bed. 'I've got the wrong bag.'

'You can't have,' said Sharon, opening hers. 'Mine's all right. And we put them on at the same time.'

I pulled out a pair of blue and red swimming trunks with a 40-inch waist label.

'Suits you,' giggled Sharon. 'They'll get you noticed all right.'

By this time, I was going all hot and cold, trying to remember what I'd packed and what might now have gone for ever. At least six expensive thick paperbacks which I'd been dying to read. A nearly-new bottle of Chanel No 5 which mum had given me for my birthday. A travelling alarm clock. A brand-new bikini which had taken several hours to find (am I the only woman whose bottom has very little in common with her top?). And a pair of flat sandals because I meant it about finding myself. I intended to explore the area which would be difficult in the more elegant shoes I had travelled in.

Instead, I had the following items in front of me. The swimming trunks (enough said). A travelling clock. Six thick blokey action-type books, including two by Robert Harris, whom I'd never read. A blank sketchpad. A rather nice cable green jersey. A pair of trainers size 11. Several T-shirts and shorts, none of which were folded particularly neatly. One of those cheap disposable cameras. A tennis racquet. And a magnetic draughts set.

There was more, as Sharon pointed out but that's as far as we got because I stopped her delving any deeper. 'Spoil-sport,' she said. 'Don't you see. It's our ideal opportunity to see how blokes tick. This one's definitely on his own; if he'd had a wife, she'd have folded those T-shirts.'

I neglected to point out that my own hadn't been folded either. Peter had been a stickler for tidiness which had been another bone of contention between us. He'd also owned a very expensive camera which he would fiddle with for hours before finally getting round to taking a picture. Pushing this thought to the back of my mind, I rang the hotel rep who said she'd do what she could to track down my missing suitcase.

'Is there a name on the one you've got?' she asked.

Naturally, I'd already checked but the piece of flimsy string hanging from the handle, suggested it had been pulled off. I only hoped the same hadn't happened to mine.

By the second day of our holiday, there was still no sign of my missing suitcase and Sharon was getting very fed up with lending me her clothes – especially as all that hassle over Peter meant that my newly-slimmed legs looked better in her designer shorts than her own did. By the third day, I was wondering why I'd never met Robert Harris before or another action-packed author whose cover I had previously ignored in bookshops.

'Do you think you ought to be reading someone else's books?' asked Sharon.

I pointed out that as the rep still hadn't been to collect the suitcase, (no wonder this was a cheap, no-frills holiday), I might as well make use of it. The green sweater even came in handy one evening when it got chilly and I rather liked the manly smell on it which was distinctly familiar in an odd sort of way. The tennis racquet also gave me ideas. Well, I wouldn't have borrowed it except that the hotel was charging a ridiculous amount to hire theirs. Besides, my suitcase owner's racquet was far less superior than the one in my own missing suitcase. Blast, that's another thing I'd forgotten was in there.

'It's a bit like Cinderella, isn't it?' I said, over a crystal-blue cocktail after a blissfully hot day by the pool.

'What do you mean?' asked Sharon crossly. She still hadn't found someone nice and there were only three days left.

'Well,' I giggled (partly on account of the said crystal-blue cocktail), 'I quite like the look of my suitcase owner from his contents. And if he's got mine, and likes the look of me, we could be a match.'

Sharon eyed me sardonically. 'Thought you didn't believe in blind dates and by the way, watch you don't splash my dress with your drink. It's dry clean only.'

I bought myself a pair of flat sandals from a local shop to go on my walks (the size 11 trainers would have dwarfed me). And by the end of the holiday, I had it all worked out. I'd chuck in my job which reminded me too much of Peter (his company often liaised with mine) and I'd put Peter down to experience. I'd start doing things for myself like learning to paint. That sketchpad had given me an idea. And no, I didn't borrow it. I just bought myself my own from the hotel shop. 'Not bad,' said Sharon surprised. 'You were always good at art, at school. Remember?'

I got out the sketchpad again at the airport when there was a five hour delay. I certainly had enough subjects to choose from, with hordes of holidaymakers sprawled over plastic chairs, waiting for their flights to be called.

'That's good,' said a small boy with a floppy brown fringe and a green cable knit jumper. 'My dad likes to draw too but he lost his sketchpad when his suitcase went missing. He's just gone to find out about it now. My name's Ben, by the way.'

I looked up. 'Was the suitcase navy blue?'

The small boy nodded seriously.

Sharon gave me one of her warning looks. It said 'Married'.

Just my luck to find the one blind date I couldn't have.

'He got someone else's suitcase instead,' said my new friend. 'A lady's. Well we think it was a lady even though her bikini bottom was much bigger than her top. He read all her books, though I said he shouldn't. We didn't touch her perfume because that was girly but we did play with her Scrabble. He said it was fair deals because someone else had our draughts board. I like games, don't you?'

'No,' said Sharon firmly, no doubt thinking of all the evenings I had beaten her with the small boy's draught set. 'Is this your dad?'

A gorgeous tall, handsome man was approaching us, with the same kind of floppy fringe as his son's. In his hand, he had a navy blue suitcase. He looked at the identical one by my side.

'Your son tells me that you lost your case on the way out,' I said. 'Me too. Do you read Robert Harris, by any chance?'

The man smiled. It was a rather nice boyish crinkly smile. 'I rather like Sebastian Faulkes now. And I'd forgotten how much I enjoyed Scrabble.'

And that was how I met Peter. Pity about the name. But as I kept telling Sharon, the two couldn't have been more different. He'd had a bad experience too; Ben's mother had been rather like the original Peter when it came to telling the truth. They'd been divorced for a couple of years now. But he had an amicable arrangement with her over Ben, which was why he took him on holiday.

The following summer, I bought a large bright orange suitcase which couldn't possibly belong to anyone else. Well, it could actually. It could belong to Peter because in fact, I bought two. They were reduced which was, as Sharon said, understandable, in view of the garish colour. Still, at least it made sure that no one else could take them by mistake. I wouldn't like to think of anyone else getting their hands on my new man.

'Do you think,' asked Ben curiously, after we'd checked in our bags, 'that if someone took my case by mistake, I might find a holiday friend like you and Dad did?'

We were still chuckling over that one as we stood in Departures, when I suddenly saw him. He'd put on a bit of weight and he'd got rid of the glasses but that expensive camera round his neck was a dead give-away.

'It's Peter,' I said horrified, looking the other way in case he saw me.

My own Peter put his arm around me. He looked worried and for a moment, exactly like the little boy who was standing next to us. 'You don't feel anything for him any more, do you?'

'Absolutely not,' I said firmly and truthfully. 'As far as I'm concerned, he's merely old baggage.'

4

Plotting Your Short Story

Plotting a short story is very different from plotting a novel. For a start, you've got less space to get a story going. That might seem obvious but it's amazing how many would-be short-story writers then forget this. It's essential to get in there and grab the reader from the beginning. With limited space, every word counts.

I am often asked how I tackle plotting. It's easy to assume that there is one magic, foolproof way but in fact, it very much depends on the kind of person you are and how you think. Below, I'm going to describe how I do it and also how other writer friends do it. After that, you need to try out different methods for yourself to see which one works best for you.

You might be surprised by finding that you're a natural with a plot method you haven't considered before.

STARTING WITH AN IDEA

This is what I do. I begin with an idea and then I go on from there. Often, all I write down in my Ideas Book, is the phrase or concept that started me thinking in the first place. For instance, I recently wrote a short story for the *Sunday Express* about a woman who cooks a meal for her ex-husband.

I thought this might be interesting because it brings in all kinds of emotions. She prepared a meal she had cooked for him many times before, when they'd been married. They would, I thought, have all kinds of things to talk about.

Developing your idea

Over the next few days, I allowed the idea time to germinate. Then I realised that it would be more interesting to start the story as though she was inviting a stranger to dinner. I could drop clues that might suggest it was a blind date. For instance, she could look at his photograph and wonder what he would think of her.

When the husband arrives, a quarter of a way through the story, we realise they are ex-husband and wife. But the plot then takes a slightly different twist. He doesn't like the meal she's cooked and when she points out it used to be his favourite, he says he's changed. He then refers to a restaurant they used to go to – which throws her because she never went there. The ex-wife then realises that he had taken someone else there when they'd been married.

The plot is beginning to develop now because she realises that she would never want to go back to him again. At this point, another idea occurred to me. Suppose the wife ran out of an important ingredient for her meal, before the husband arrived? She'd do what we all do, wouldn't she? In other words, borrow from a neighbour.

Adding a twist

It was here that I found another twist coming into my head. Suppose I made the reader think that the neighbour was a woman when in fact, it was a man. I then racked my brains for a name that wouldn't give the game away and came up with 'Mel'. Mel not only provided the odd ingredient but also gave her advice.

So, during the meal, our heroine keeps recalling advice which Mel has given her. By the time we get to the final course, she's had enough. She sees off the ex-husband without coffee and goes round to her neighbour to report on the evening. And that's when we find out that Mel is really a man – and a rather attractive one at that! You can read the full story at the end of this chapter.

You can see from this that I started off with an idea which grew and also changed along the way. I didn't have a skeleton plot on paper but I did have lots of points in my head. I also wrote a few down but not many.

This is just one way of doing it. Below, I've listed some others.

USING INDEX CARDS
Buy yourself a pack of different coloured index cards. Use each colour to represent a character. Plot your story according to what each character does on the relevant coloured card.

The advantage of this is that it makes you focus on each character and the part he or she plays in the plot. It also means you keep your notes in a tidy way.

The disadvantages are that this method does require you to work out a substantial amount beforehand although you can add bits along the way.

USING A WHITEBOARD
If you're lucky enough to have a room of your own in which to write, put up a whiteboard or cork board with pins on it. Use this to write down notes for your short story and even a mind map.

Mind maps are much simpler than they sound! Start with one word or one phrase in the middle. For example, if you think of the story I've just mentioned, you could write SPECIAL MEAL.

Then draw a line from the circle and at the end, another circle with EX-HUSBAND COMES TO SUPPER. Then another line from the circle with the phrase READER THINKS IT'S A BLIND DATE. And so on.

This might appeal to you if you have a visual memory. As you look at it, other ideas might come to you and you can add or erase as you please.

THE A–Z METHOD

This is simply writing down a list of events in the story you intend to write. The method suits people who feel more comfortable and secure if they have what I call a 'knitting pattern' in front of them. They know exactly what they're going to do and that gives them confidence.

The big disadvantage, as far as I'm concerned, is that you need to work it all out beforehand. This means you haven't given your imagination a chance to change. If you suddenly feel that a character should do something different, you might feel tempted to stop it from doing that because it doesn't conform to your original plan.

So if you do opt for this method, try to be open to ideas which come to you while writing and don't think you have to stay with your original concept. After all, if a character is realistic, it will change and 'tell' you things you didn't know about before.

GETTING THE RIGHT PACE

Thinking up a plot is one thing. But making sure that it has the right kind of pace, is another.

What exactly is pace? Imagine you are walking very slowly through some woods. You can see the flowers and notice tiny details like twigs snapping but it might not be very exciting. Now start to walk a little faster. You are beginning to breathe slightly faster and might, as a result, meet someone you wouldn't have met if you'd continued at your original snail pace. Now walk very fast. It's getting more exciting, isn't it? Especially if you knock into another walker without meaning to. Now run. You're out of breath and you don't know where you're going.

Writing a short story (and novel) is a bit like this. For a good read (and good walk), you need a mixture of slow walking, jogging and running. In other words, you need to allow the reader some time to reflect and some time to get excited about what is happening to the character and the plot.

THE TREE DIAGRAM

But how can you check you've got the right balance between that quiet time and the active time in your story? This is where a tree diagram comes in.

EXERCISE

I want you to recall the story of 'Little Red Riding Hood'. Now draw a straight vertical line down the centre of the page. Along it, sideways, write LITTLE RED RIDING HOOD. What is the first thing that happens in the story? It's when Little Red Riding Hood's mother tells her to visit her grandmother. So draw a branch at the bottom of the tree, going upwards towards the top right corner, and write RR TOLD TO VISIT GRANDMOTHER.

Now draw a line above that and write RR MEETS WOLF. Then another branch and write WOLF GOES TO GRANDMOTHER'S HOUSE. And so on. Start going down the left hand side of the tree with all the different stages of action in the story and finish off with WOODCUTTER KILLS WOLF AND SAVES GRANNY AND RED RIDING HOOD.

Take a good look at your tree. There should be a good mixture of reflective times and action moments. Reflective times include Red Riding Hood walking through the wood or telling her grandmother she looks different. Action times include the Wolf running to the grandmother's house and then eating her up. And it does exactly that! Which partly explains why this tale has been so successful over the years.

When you've written your story, it helps to do a tree diagram just like this. Make sure you have enough happening and that you have a combination of active and thoughtful times.

THE PARAGRAPH GAME

Another way of checking pace is to make sure that something different happens every four or five paragraphs. When I mean 'something different', I mean there ought to be a change of gear. One of the characters needs to go to a different place or make a discovery or talk to someone else.

If, on the other hand, you spend several paragraphs on a character who is constantly moaning to himself or others without doing anything, the plot is going to flag.

READING IT THROUGH

Always read your work out loud. If you get to a point where you yourself feel a bit bored, change it! If you think it's boring, chances are that you're right. Don't tell yourself that it doesn't matter because the interesting bit is coming along soon. You'll have lost your reader by then!

EXERCISE

◆ Go back to your ideas list. Select one of them and write a tree diagram for the plot.

◆ Make sure you have a good mixture of action and reflective periods.

—— **Eating In** ——
by Sophie King
(this story was first published in the *Sunday Express* magazine)

She'd prepared this meal so many times that she could do it in her sleep. Smoked salmon for starters. Cannelloni. Chocolate mousse. Perhaps she should have tried something more adventurous but she wouldn't go wrong with this. And it was important – so important – that this evening went to plan.

Julia laid the slices of salmon neatly out onto the serving dish before washing her hands and opening the unsealed envelope. Pathetic, she knew, but she couldn't resist sneaking one more look at the photograph he'd sent.

'A handsome man,' she said out loud. 'Not young but then again, nor am I any more. Nice smile. Crinkly blue eyes. Shortish hair that looks as though it's just been combed.'

What, she wondered as she melted the butter for the cannelloni cheese sauce, would he make of her? Glancing in the kitchen mirror, she automatically tossed back her shoulder-length hair which was still on the right side of honey, thanks to the hairdresser. Quite well preserved (that sounded like the jam she used to make when the children were small!) although it was a pity about the shadows under her eyes. Still, as her neighbour Mel had said, what else did she expect after everything?

Mind you, she thought with a frisson of excitement as she popped the cannelloni into the oven, tonight might well be the start of something new even though, as Mel had pointed out, she was taking a risk. Taking risks wasn't something that she, Julia, did. Which was precisely why she'd made the chocolate mousse last night so it was already waiting in the fridge. Waiting, like her.

The sitting room looked neat and tidy thanks to her frantic efforts this morning. All she had to do now was get dressed. Sifting through the wardrobe, she told herself off for not having decided this earlier. Should it be the blue dress which reminded her of the cornflowers in Devon or a nice safe pair of black trousers? Julia felt anything but safe.

The doorbell! He was early. Slipping into the blue dress and fastening it up as she went, Julia almost tripped downstairs. Opening it, her first thought was that Ben had lost his tan from the photo.

'Hello.' He smiled uncertainly at her, as though they were strangers. 'How are you doing?'

She found herself nodding over-enthusiastically. 'Really great. Come on through. Supper's ready. I made your favourite.'

But he was still standing in the hall, looking at some photographs of the children she'd taken last summer. 'They're great. Could I have copies?'

'Sure. Have you seen them yet?'

'No. You?'

Julia took out the cannelloni which was looking crisp round the edge, just the way he liked it. 'Emily came down to lunch last Sunday. She's got a new boyfriend – nicer than the last.'

They each smiled wryly and for a second, there was a glimmer of those years they had shared together; the daughters they had made. 'I like your dress,' he said suddenly. 'The blue reminds me of those flowers in Devon.'

So he remembered their last holiday!

'Cornflowers. And thanks for the photograph.' Her hands shaking, she began opening the bottle of Californian wine, another of their old favourites. He reached over to do it for her and his hands brushed hers, sending tremors down her spine.

'Just thought you might like to see what Sydney is like. We took that in the botanical gardens.'

We? Julia sat down opposite him, trying not to look at her ex-husband. It had been so long now. Five years and eight months since he'd emigrated after the divorce. And now he was back to see his mother, which was why he'd come round for supper 'just for old times' sake.'

Ben was picking at the salmon, pushing a piece to one side.

'Something wrong?'

'Sorry. There's just too much pepper on it, that's all.'

'But you always used to like it that way.'

He shrugged. 'Did I?'

Getting up to hide her face, she said, 'But you still like cannelloni, don't you? I made it specially.'

'Great. Remember how we always had it at the Italian restaurant in Covent Garden?'

She frowned. 'Did we?'

He coloured and with a pang she realised he must have gone with someone else.

'How about you, Julia.' He topped up her glass. 'Are you happy?'

'Yes. I've still got my job at the library and Emily isn't far away and ...'

She stopped as his hand closed over hers. 'I've missed you.'

Had he really said that or had she imagined it? It was exactly how she'd dreamt it, ever since he'd left. But now, watching him talking while he ate (a habit she'd always hated), she wasn't sure any more. As Mel said, she'd made her own life now with its Salsa dancing classes, book group, telly suppers, doing what she wanted without anyone criticising her.

Whoops!

'I'm so sorry!' Springing up, she desperately tried to mop up the red wine that was seeping over his white shirt leaving an angry red mark like the blotch across his face.

'It's ruined! Didn't you see my glass?'

'I said I'm sorry.'

He nodded tightly. 'Forget it.'

Ten minutes later, she found herself knocking at Mel's door. 'How did it go then?'

A pair of handsome blue eyes looked at her and Julia wobbled. 'Fantastic. You were right. It was a shock seeing him again but it's proved I'm over him. Besides, I'm much happier on my own.'

'Really?' Mel – short for Melvin – raised a pair of thick, bushy eyebrows.

'Well...,' she hesitated, looking down at the chocolate mousse. 'You wouldn't like to share this with me, would you?'

He grinned. A broad, generous, warm grin that melted her body like cannelloni sauce. 'That will do – at least for starters.'

And as she followed him in, Julia began planning a whole new menu...

5

Viewpoint: Whose Shoes are you Standing In?

Have you ever read a book where you felt as though you were being told to go in all kinds of different directions? I'm not just talking plot here. I mean the kind of book that encourages you to see things from one character's point of view and then suddenly makes you switch allegiances or sides by presenting the situation from someone else's perspective?

This is called 'confusing viewpoint' and is to be avoided at all costs! It's a particular sin in a short story where there is less space to get it right. In fact, if you don't, the worst thing will happen. The reader will merely turn the page and move on to something which doesn't confuse them.

WHAT EXACTLY IS VIEWPOINT?

Imagine you are at a party. You are standing in a pair of comfortable shoes which also match your outfit. You are observing everyone else chatting. The woman over there has got pink lipstick on her teeth although she doesn't seem to be aware of it. The man she is talking to is mopping his forehead with a large white handkerchief as though it is very hot, even though you are feeling a little chilly in your sleeveless dress.

Now imagine you are the woman with lipstick on her teeth. You are feeling very hungry because you thought food would be

73

provided at this party and it hasn't been. The man you are talking to has just got over a bad dose of 'flu – or so he has just told you – which is why he is mopping his forehead. You are desperately hoping you are not going to catch it. There's a woman across the room whom you vaguely recognise and who is wearing a rather old-fashioned pair of shoes which matches her outfit in colour but not in style.

Now imagine you are a man and feeling rather ill. You're beginning to wish you hadn't come to this party at all and stayed in bed which is where you have been for the past few days. But you promised the hostess – who happens to be a woman you rather admire – to be there and you didn't want to let her down. You are talking to a woman with lipstick on her teeth who clearly isn't interested in what you are saying and is dying to get away. But there is a rather nice woman on the other side of the room whom you'd rather talk to. She's rather short although that might be because she's wearing flat shoes unlike all the other women in the room.

Understanding different viewpoints

Above, you have three different viewpoints. Each one could work as the beginning of a story in its own right. But if you started with the woman with flat shoes and then in the second or third paragraph, moved on to the woman with lipstick on her teeth and then, in the sixth or seventh paragraph, described what the man with the handkerchief was feeling, you would leave the reader wondering what was going on.

Do you see what I mean? To spell it out, it's fine to describe what other people are like from one person's perspective. But if you then try to get into the skin of a different person every few paragraphs, it's confusing viewpoint.

WHOSE SHOES ARE YOU STANDING IN?

Another way of looking at it is to imagine you are standing in your character's shoes. They are a magic pair of shoes which mean you can only guess at other people's internal thoughts instead of knowing what they definitely are.

Let's give a name to the woman in flat shoes. We'll call her Angie. Now let's imagine her thoughts. 'I wonder if that man with the white handkerchief realises I'm here,' she thought to herself.

It's fine to wonder what someone is thinking or doing or – as in the above example – realises. We all do that. We all make surmises about someone on the train or someone in the office or someone we know quite well. But it wouldn't work if the next paragraph immediately jumped in with the man thinking 'That it! I remember that woman now. I met her the other month at the Morrison's.'

Every time you're worried about viewpoint, remember those shoes. Ease your feet into them and look at the rest of the world through your magic shoes.

EXCEPTIONS TO THE RULE

There are, of course, exceptions to every rule and here is one of them. A big one.

It's perfectly acceptable to write different viewpoints providing you give a clear sign to the reader that you are doing so. How do you do this? There are two main ways. Either you can start a new chapter with a different character's viewpoint. Or you can leave a considerable amount of white space between the two different attitudes.

Of course, with a short story, you have no option. You do not have the luxury of space to insert chapters. But never mind. You can allow yourself two or three lines of white space, providing that is that you are writing a longer short story. For example, 1,500 words upwards.

Any shorter and – in my view – you would make the reader jump around too much. But you can get away with it in a longer story.

PROS AND CONS

I think you can have great fun with multi-character viewpoints in a short story. Those of you who have read my novels, will know that this is one of my trade marks. I generally have three or four main characters but each one will express their viewpoint in a different chapter.

They see each other and comment on each other, of course. But that is one of the beauties of different viewpoints. We can find out something about a character which we didn't know before.

Exactly the same can happen with multi-viewpoint characters in short stories. It gives you a window into the minds of other characters and – just as vital in a short story – it can move the plot along nicely.

Using multi-viewpoints

Let me give you an example. I once wrote a short story called 'After You'. It started with a driver who always set out for work at the same time every day. She let someone in front of her at the traffic lights. As a result, the driver of the car got to his destination a little earlier. He then met someone else as a result and . . . well I'll leave that your imagination.

The story was divided into three parts. Each one showed the viewpoint from three people yet they were all linked because wittingly or unwittingly, their paths had crossed.

I sometimes think life is like an electric circuit. We go round and round but our paths are affected by the people who switch us on and off or whom we try to avoid or home in on.

HOW VIEWPOINT CAN IMPROVE THE PLOT

Different viewpoints can broaden the canvas of your plot. It can allow you to go to different places which one character wouldn't be able to do on his or her own. I wrote another story in which a woman looked out of the window and saw someone walking by. I then followed the life of the man walking by and then of someone else whom he met. And so on.

The important thing is to find a situation where you can tie it up neatly at the end. Ideally, each character needs to have solved his or her own problem in a very short space of time. This isn't easy but it can be done providing you move the action along and don't spend too much time dwelling on characters' internal thoughts.

SUMMARY

◆ See the story from one character's point of view, although there are exceptions.

◆ Imagine that pair of imaginary shoes.

◆ If you're going to have a multi-viewpoint story, make sure you signal this to the reader through white space.

EXERCISE

◆ Think of ideas that would make a multi-viewpoint story.

◆ Write 'Little Red Riding Hood' from the wolf's point of view. Here's the first paragraph to get you going.

The wolf was going for a walk through the woods when he suddenly heard a woman speaking inside a cottage. 'Little Red Riding Hood,' he heard the voice saying. 'I want you to take this lovely basket of cookies to your grandmother.'

'Cookies?' The wolf's ears pricked up. He loved cookies and besides, he was feeling very hungry.

The following story appeared in *Woman's Weekly* and will, I hope, give you an example of viewpoint. The reader sees the story through Eileen's eyes although there are other characters too.

—— The Button Box ——
by Sophie King

Eileen Mills held up the blue button to the light. She could see it now, as clearly as when she had bought it all those years ago, from the haberdashers with the wooden shelves and upside-down brass, shell handles. She had only been a child, maybe nine or perhaps ten, but even in those days, she had loved sewing.

'Another dress for your doll?' Miss Molly would ask, smiling that bright smile which lit up her face and almost stopped you noticing that nasty scar above her lip. Her mother called it a hare lip but Eileen couldn't understand what that had to do with the hares or rabbits that played in the field at the bottom of her garden.

That's where Eileen liked to sew in the summer. She'd sit in the little hut that her father had built her and cut out patterns from left-over scraps of material which Miss Molly kept for her mother, calling them remnants. Remnants seemed a dull sort of word for the pretty cottons which Molly snipped at, with the pinking shears that her mother had bought her for Christmas. Once, Miss Molly had saved her a beautiful piece of bright blue silk but to her disappointment, it had slipped all over the place when she tried to cut it. It was even worse when Eileen attempted to sew a button on. Her needle kept tearing at the material which, although pretty, was something called floored even though her mother said it was spelt a different way.

To make her feel better, her mother had bought her an exquisite set of mother of pearl buttons on a white card with 3d written in Miss Molly's lovely, curvy writing at the top. 3d was two weeks' pocket money in those days but because of the silk disappointment, her mother had treated her. How she had loved those buttons, Eileen thought to herself. They were far too beautiful to actually use. Instead, she would keep them in the wooden carved box which her uncle Gerald had brought all the way back from India. Every now and then, when her baby brother was asleep and less likely to try and grab something which didn't belong to him, she would take out the card of mother of pearl buttons and watch them glint. Then Eileen would close her eyes and imagine where they had come from. Her mother had said they were made in India, where the box had come from. But she knew better. Someone, maybe a little girl of about her age, had found them in the sand when looking for shells. There had been six of them, almost the same shape but very slightly different, like this one which had a funny little dent on the edge.

Eileen kept her treasure box under her bed in the room she shared with Philip. Then, one day, an ordinary little brown button fell off her school skirt when she took it off one evening. 'No point in sewing it on again,' said her mother. 'That skirt was too small for you anyway. We'll buy another for the new term. Keep the button in your button box. It might come in useful.'

Eileen hadn't thought of her treasure box as a button box but it made sense. Her mother had a button box which was heavy with all kinds of buttons, like pebbles. Most were round but there were some exciting shapes too like the beige rectangular one that looked like a miniature farm gate and was really a buckle but had sneaked into the button box by mistake. Eileen's favourite was a tiny white rabbit button which her mother had told her she had worn on her very first cardigan, soon after she'd been born. 'You can have it, if you like,' her mother said one day, 'for your collection.' And Eileen knew that when she had her own child, she would sew it on his or her cardigan, just like her mother had on hers.

As she got older, Eileen's sewing skills grew with her. By the time she was twelve, she could easily cut out quite complicated dress patterns, using the flimsy thin paper outlines with little crosses down the sides, that she bought from Miss Molly. Eileen would spend hours looking at the elegant figures of the women who featured on the cover of these patterns. It wasn't always easy to see what kind of buttons they had on their flowing jackets or skirts which seemed to billow out with the kind of elegance that you didn't normally see outside Miss Molly's shop. But if Eileen couldn't see them, she would imagine them. A brilliant green button for that jacket and a sparkling silver one for the bridesmaid dress which she had been allowed to make for cousin Maggy's wedding.

Eileen was very excited about Maggy's wedding. At 14, she had despaired of ever being a bridesmaid but that was mainly because no one in her family had got married for ages. Her mother had said that was because of the war and that she hoped no one would stare too much at poor Maggy's Philip in his wheelchair. Eileen hoped they wouldn't either. She liked Philip who had a kind smile and had had two perfectly good legs when she had last seen him.

In the event, no one need have worried. Maggy looked beautiful in the dress she had made herself and everyone said it must run in the family because Eileen's bridesmaid dress, was also beautiful. 'What exquisite buttons,' said one of Philip's aunts when she examined the tiny, fine stitching afterwards. 'Aren't you a clever girl?'

Eileen had secretly kept one of the spare silver buttons to put in her button box. And Maggy had given her the tiny white ball of a button which did up one of the many loops at the side of her dress. She had also thrown the bouquet straight at Eileen so she had no option but to catch it, amidst much blushing and laughter. To her embarrassment, George, Philip's younger cousin, was standing next to her at the time.

'Well caught,' he said admiringly. 'Something tells me you're good at games.'

And Eileen, who had been too busy sewing all her life to pick up so much as a lacrosse stick, wondered whether it was time to spread her interests. She kept her button box going, of course but she also learned to play tennis under the kindly supervision of George and his mother Pammy, who lived in the neighbouring village. And when Pammy's tennis skirt threatened to fall down after a particularly energetic shot, Eileen just happened to have a spare button and thread in her bag. 'What a sensible girl,' Pammy later said to her son, meaningfully. 'And pretty too.'

Eileen and George were married just before her nineteenth birthday. As a wedding present, her mother gave her a new sewing machine. 'You'll need it before long,' she said, with a knowing look.

Eileen spent her first pregnancy doing what she liked best, now she could no longer play tennis. Everyone admired the neat pile of crocheted shawls and tiny little baby jackets with the beautiful white buttons, because she didn't like to choose between blue and pink. The rabbit button was at the top, in pride of place.

When she came back from the hospital, empty-handed and dry-eyed after crying all her tears away, the first thing that Eileen did was to pick up her needle. 'It makes me think of something else,' she said to George. This time, she didn't make quite so many jackets before she was rushed to hospital again, some months before she was meant to have been. And it was a couple of months before she could bring herself to open the button box and tell herself she would give it one more go.

There was a bit of a black period after that, during which Eileen failed to call in at Miss Molly's for several months. By the time she went back, Miss Molly had sold up and there was a new shop, which called itself Spinning a Yarn and sold more wools than fabric. Its collection of buttons was very poor but it didn't matter. Well-wishers, unsure how to show their sympathy, often dropped off buttons for Eileen's collection just in case she felt like sewing again. Susie Martin suggested that, while she was waiting, how would she feel about making a dress for an important dinner that Susie had to go to. Someone else then asked for a skirt and suddenly, before Eileen knew it, she had built up a small, select number of customers even though her stomach remained slightly rounded but totally empty.

By the time George went off to fight in the war which everyone thought would never happen again, they had got over their disappointment. They had each other, they told themselves and Eileen had her little business. When George failed to come back, Eileen shut herself in her room for some weeks until emerging to continue her life almost as she had done before. This time, she had one more button in her box; a brass button from George's regimental suit which they had sent back to her. It was the one part of her beloved husband which no one could take away.

'Simply dreadful,' moaned Virginia Hamble who used to be at school with Eileen and was now planning her teenage daughter's wedding. 'I really need something nice to wear and I can't bear the thought of a trip to London. I don't suppose you have anything, do you Eileen with all those bits and pieces of yours.'

Eileen did and something inside her offered to run up Virginia a rather clever little couture suit with fetching rose buttons that looked quite real. After that, Dinah from the pub asked if she would make her a skirt, not too smart but not too casual either. It sort of snowballed from there and every time there were some buttons left over, Eileen put them into her button box which was almost overflowing until her mother, no spring chicken herself, donated hers.

She took both boxes with her of course, when her arthritis took over and everything else seemed to give up. They were very good in the home, about letting her bring her most precious possessions, thought Eileen, holding up the mother of pearl button to the light, to make sure that she had the right one. It was as beautiful as it had been the day she bought it and Clare thought so too.

'What a lovely button,' she said, admiring it in the old lady's knarled palm. 'Do you know, when I was younger, I thought they came from the beach.'

'So did I,' laughed Eileen. 'And look at this. Have you ever seen such a sparkling blue in your life?'

'That's lovely,' said Clare, squatting down to the old lady's side and together they went through Eileen's box of memories. This was from the wedding where she had met her husband and this was from her niece's christening when she had made the gown.

Eileen liked Clare. She was much nicer than Zoe who was always turning up the television and putting her box of buttons away. 'What's the point of her looking at them when she can't even see, any more?' she'd say to Clare. Clare knew there was no point in trying to explain. Mrs Mills might be blind now, but that didn't mean she couldn't see her memories. With that in mind, Eileen certainly wouldn't have liked it if she had known it was Zoe who came in that morning when she'd fallen asleep for a quick snooze before lunch. 'Clare, quick,' Zoe yelled out.

Clare took one look at the old lady and knew exactly what had happened. Gently she held her friend's cool hand and somehow, she wasn't surprised when she found a large brass button inside it. It also seemed perfectly normal to find a small white button in the shape of a rabbit, sitting under the cushion of Mrs Mills' chair, as though she had left it there, especially for her.

Clare kept the button carefully until her own baby daughter was born six months later. When little Eileen grew too big for the cardigan, she snipped off the rabbit and put it in her button box, an old Christmas biscuit tin. After all, she thought, she might not be able to sew much herself. But you never knew when it might come in useful.

6

Who's Speaking Please?

HOW TO WRITE MAGAZINE DIALOGUE

'What would you say the most important thing is to get right in short stories?' I asked a writer friend of mine, Rosemary Morris recently.

Her answer was swift. 'Plenty of dialogue. It's what fiction editors look for.'

She's right. It's not the only thing they're looking for of course but dialogue has become more and more important in recent years, both in novels and in particular short stories. Why? Because, as any fiction editor will tell you, today's reader has less time to read. We all lead such busy lives that a short story is usually read in between some other activity such as getting to work, looking after children, having a coffee break and so on.

The good news about this change in our social habits is that readers might well pick up a short story instead of a novel because they feel it's less time consuming. They might also expect an 'easy read'. In fact, this is exactly why some people don't read magazine stories – because they assume it will be too easy.

Our job as short-story writers is therefore to please both camps. We want our stories to be readable. But we also want them to be challenging and interesting.

START TALKING NOW

So how does dialogue fit into this? For a start (and I mean this literally), dialogue can draw us straight into a story at the beginning. Providing, that is, that the dialogue is intriguing enough for us to want to carry on.

> *'You'll never guess what John did yesterday,' said Julia.*
>
> *'I don't want to know,' replied her sister. 'He's out of my life for good now.'*

Mmmmm. When I wrote the first line, I hadn't thought of the last few words in the second until I got there. In fact, I thought I was in danger of producing a 'How to write boring dialogue' sentence. But the fact that John is out of Julia's sister's life for good now, is slightly intriguing isn't it? If only because we suspect that the opposite is true.

We have now set the scene for something to happen. We'd rather like to know what John did now. And we're wondering why Julia is telling her sister. Is she trying to spur her on out of kindness? Or is she causing trouble? Sisters can be great combinations of character, can't they?

Or how about this?

> *'Put that back immediately,' instructed Susie.*
>
> *'Why?' Ben looked up. 'They'll never miss it.'*

Really? Could Ben be doing something he shouldn't? Or is he within his rights? Either way, we want to know a bit more about

WHO'S SPEAKING PLEASE? / **87**

the situation. So we read on. And that, after all, means we've crossed our first hurdle.

WHO'S SPEAKING – AND WHY?

Although dialogue is vital, don't make the common mistake of getting so much into the swing that the first half of your page is all chit chat. If we don't know who is talking or what the situation is about, we lose interest. Fast.

We therefore need to know by the third or fourth paragraph, more about John and Julia and Julia's sister (whom, you'll notice, should have acquired a name by now). We also need to know where Susie and Ben are. You might know they're mother and son – but does the reader? Or you might want them to be slightly confused at this stage.

On the other hand, we don't want to know too much as you will remember from the Chapter 4 on plot, where I explained that you can't tell everything immediately. Instead, you need to tease out the information rather like a roll of cotton wool so the reader is kept on his or her toes.

And this is where dialogue can play its part. We can use it to help delay the final outcome. We can use it to perpetuate any confusion or misunderstanding between the characters which might form part of the plot. And we can use it to show how a character develops or solves his or her own problem.

WE DON'T JUST TALK

When you're talking to someone, you don't just sit or stand there, do you? You normally do something at the same time. I'm a real multi-tasking culprit. I'll have long conversations with friends while I'm unloading the dishwasher or cleaning the kitchen floor or putting on my make up. It plays havoc with my neck to crane the phone between my ear and my shoulder but I lead a busy life and I wouldn't get things done otherwise.

If your characters are to be real people, they will do the same – or something similar. They might not be rude enough to type while they are talking (another occasional failing of mine, I'm afraid) but they are bound to run their hands through their hair; dry up while chatting to someone else in the kitchen; open post; and maybe chat to a friend (a good friend) in the bath. In fact, there are all kinds of things people could do while talking either on the phone or face to face.

Imagine for example, that Julia is doing something while she is talking to her sister. Does it make it more interesting? Here's an example:

> *'You'll never guess what John did yesterday,' said Julia as she climbed up the ladder.*

There's another dimension now, isn't there? Why is Julia climbing the ladder? Will it push the plot forward? Could she fall off? Or could her sister be so upset at what Julia is telling her that she falls against the ladder accidentally and sends her sister flying? The opportunities are endless and all because we have slipped in a small piece of action.

EXERCISE

Write a list of actions that people could be doing while talking to someone on the phone or face to face.

HOW MUCH IS TOO MUCH?

We're writing short stories here, remember. So the amount of dialogue might vary from the amount needed in a novel. Most of the fiction editors I spoke to, agreed that they looked for around 70 per cent of dialogue in a short story.

This is quite a lot, isn't it? The reason is, as we've already said, to engage the reader's interest and make them feel this isn't a difficult read. Psychologically, the amount of white space helps too. If a reader looks at a page and sees a dense mass of text, it's off-putting.

This is also another reason for putting in plenty of new paragraphs. And do remember that you need a new paragraph every time a person speaks or does something.

Of course, as always, there are exceptions to the rule. You're probably all picking up published short stories and working out that there isn't as much dialogue as 70 per cent. But you certainly need 60 per cent upwards.

This percentage also includes what I call internal dialogue. In other words, when the heroine (or hero) is talking to herself. People often get confused about the use of speech marks here. Do they need them or not?

In fact, it depends on the style of the magazine and also the clarity of the piece. I tend not to put in speech marks for internal talk because I feel my sentences are normally clear enough. Here's an example.

I can't tell her, thought Julia, as she reached for the paint brush. Not the truth, at any rate.

The 'thought Julia' makes it plain that this is speech which she herself is thinking.

A BIT MORE GRAMMAR

Talking of grammar, remember that you need to put the comma or full stop after the end of the sentence but before the speech marks. For example:

'I'd like to know what John did last night,' protested Julia's sister.

Think of it as the speech mark tucking up the comma into bed. If you have an exclamation mark, you don't need a comma or full stop. For example:

'Put that down!' shouted Ben's mother.

Should you have double speech marks or single? This depends on the magazine's style so examine each one carefully. *Woman's Weekly* for example, likes double speech marks so that if someone is then using reported speech, it can be shown by single marks. Here's an example:

"When I met John, he said 'Oh it's you,'" admitted Julia.

Here you will see that the 'Oh it's you' belongs to John but Julia is recalling it in what is known as reported speech. This is because she is reporting what he said.

DIALOGUE DOESN'T HAVE TO BE SPOKEN

Dialogue can also come across in text messages, e-mails and answerphone messages. Make full use of this – it helps to relieve the monotony of ordinary dialogue on the page and it can be a short way of moving the plot forward in a short story.

MORE ABOUT VIEWPOINT

Yes, I know we've covered this in the previous chapter but remember it when writing your dialogue. The following paragraph is an example.

> *Julia climbed down the ladder, hoping she wasn't going to be spotted, and brushed away her sister's offer of help. 'It's fine, thanks. I can manage.'*
>
> *Her sister felt a flicker of irritation. Why was Julia always so independent, she thought to herself.*

The above two paragraphs show two different people's train of thoughts. Julia is hoping she wouldn't be spotted. Her sister feels a flicker of irritation. How can we jump so easily from one person's head to another?

If, however, we took out the 'hoping she wasn't going to be spotted', we might have got away with it because an observer could have noted her brushing away her sister's offer of help. We wouldn't need to be in her skin, or indeed her shoes, to see that.

CAN YOU HEAR THE VOICE?

If you've followed the advice in the chapter on characterisation, you will hopefully have made sure your dialogue reflects the kind of person you are portraying. For instance, a worrier might constantly worry in his or her dialogue. Someone who is always optimistic or indeed pessimistic will also reveal that in his or her speech. For example, 'Isn't it a wonderful day?'

It's very important that your dialogue continues the voice of your character. Not only does it make that character come to life but it also removes the need to constantly say who is speaking. If, for instance, Julia is always the kind of person to worry, we might know it is her in the following paragraph.

'I do hope John is all right. He looked awfully pale.'

'Of course he is,' snapped her sister. 'He's always that colour.'

As I said in Chapter 3, we can make characters come alive by giving them their own phrases and mannerisms. You can also give someone's dialogue a voice by providing them with what I call a 'trademark phrase'. This is a sentence or group of words which he or she often uses. We all know people who are always saying the same thing, don't we?

Here are some examples:

Mustn't grumble.
You know.
Wait a minute.
See what I mean, like?

Try adding your own words to this list and then drop them in to your character's speech. You don't want to do it too often or it loses its impact. But it can be a very useful way to identify your speaker especially in a short story where space is limited.

ALTERNATIVES TO 'SAID'

Since a short story needs to contain so much dialogue, it's important to think of other ways of saying 'he said'. Some people think it doesn't matter and that if you have lots of 'he said' and 'she said', it eventually washes over the reader so he or she doesn't feel it's too repetitious.

However, although this might be true in a novel, I believe it's less so in a short story where there are fewer words on a page. So try thinking of alternatives. Here's a list to get you going:

Whispered	Smiled
Sniggered	Yelled
Hissed	Cried, etc.
Laughed	

ACCENT

You can also identify a character in dialogue by giving him or her an accent. However, do so with care! Only do this if you are sure you have got the accent exactly right. You might need to do some research on this by interviewing someone from the area if you are not from it yourself. Otherwise, you are bound to get a reader from the place you are depicting who will feel the accent isn't right. And then you'll lose credibility.

If you're going to have the kind of speech where a character omits the 't' for example, you need to be consistent throughout his or her dialogue. And that can be very hard work.

One way out, is to say: 'John always dropped his t's when talking which Julia found highly irritating.' That way, you have set the scene although you will still need to put in the occasional example yourself.

Another way is to say: 'John spoke in what he fondly thought was a West Yorkshire accent'. This is rather amusing because it says something about John if he has to pretend to have an accent. It also allows for errors if the accent isn't spot on.

SUMMARY

- ◆ Short stories need lots of dialogue – possibly up to 70 per cent.
- ◆ Dialogue needs to be used to move on the plot.
- ◆ Insert action between dialogue.
- ◆ Make sure your dialogue has a voice.

EXERCISE

Choose one of your plots from an earlier chapter. Now write the opening dialogue between two or more characters, using the points we've discussed.

The following story, which has some examples of dialogue, first appeared in *The Sunday Express*. I thought of it when I was on a train recently with some teenagers who were rather excited. It wasn't until part of the way through the journey that I realised they were coming back from a birthday party. And it wasn't until the end, that I realised they knew someone else in the carriage. I won't say who, or it will give the game away. But it shows that the simplest of scenes in life can be used for a short story.

—— Other People's Children ——
by Sophie King

The children on the seats next to me, were so noisy that my head was ringing. There were six of them, all laughing and jumping around like 12-year-old girls do. It was clearly a birthday party and one of them – the loudest – was excitedly unwrapping her presents on the train.

'Ooooh, that's soooo cool!' she screamed, waving around a lurid pair of electric-blue undies that didn't seem very suitable for a girl of that age. 'Thanks a bunch, Kerry!'

Kerry pulled them from her and stood up, twirling the bra bit around on her hand. It nearly smacked me in the face.

'Mind out,' sniggered one of the girls.

That was it. I stood up and moved to a seat behind, next to a grey-haired lady wearing a navy blue cardigan. 'I'm not surprised you couldn't stay there,' she sniffed. 'Children today simply don't know how to behave. Where are their parents? That's what I'd like to know. Then again, they probably wouldn't care anyway. Parents simply don't have the control any more.'

I got out my magazine which I'd been dying to read for ages and wished my new neighbour would be quiet. She was almost worse than the girls. 'They do seem rather lively,' I admitted. 'Still, it looks as though it's a birthday party. They're just over-excited.'

'Over-excited?' The woman sniffed again. 'They're running wild. Just look at them. I'm surprised the ticket collector didn't say something. They'll be swinging from the roof next.'

That was a bit of an exaggeration but the noise was pretty overpowering. One of them had started singing along to her iPod and another was on her mobile saying 'Shhh, I can't hear.'

Just as well there was no one else in the carriage.

I snuggled down into my seat and opened my magazine for some peace. Some hope.

'When I was a child,' said my grey-haired companion, tucking away her book of wordsearches into her bag, 'we wouldn't have dared behave like that. Our mothers would have sent us to our room. But nowadays, you can't even smack them. Firm discipline. That's what these children need.'

Luckily, at that point, the man with the drinks trolley came through. I bought myself a nice cup of tea and a chocolate biscuit because I felt I deserved one. The woman next to me got out her thermos and clingfilmed cheese sandwich which she ate with her beady eyes disapprovingly fixed on the birthday crowd. I almost felt sorry for them.

'Ohhh, drinks!' yelled one of the girls behind me. 'Mum gave me some money. Let's have a coke each.'

'And some crisps,' called out another.

The grey-haired lady carefully folded up her clingfilm and drew an apple out of her bag which she polished with her handkerchief. 'Additives,' she announced, before taking a bite. 'That's the root cause of all this terrible behaviour. Coke and crisps indeed! If those girls' mothers fed them sensibly, they wouldn't be clambering all over the seats.'

That wasn't quite true, I thought as I turned round to look. The girl with hooped earrings was just trying to get past one of the others to reach the trolley. But unfortunately, she jolted my disapproving neighbour's back as she did so.

'Careful,' snapped the woman. 'You almost made me spill my coffee.'

'Sorry,' called out the girl and the others erupted into giggles. Someone whispered and another one said 'What did you say?' There was another silence and then a big giggle. Clearly, they were talking about us.

My companion screwed back the lid of her thermos and carefully put her apple core into the plastic bag. 'No respect for their elders. That's their trouble. Just look at the mess they've left on the floor.'

The girl with the hooped earrings must have heard that and to her credit, she bent down and picked up the crisp packet. Then there was another whisper and yet another giggle.

Feeling rather uncomfortable, I went back to my magazine.

'Aren't you going to open MY present, Julie?' demanded one of the girls. Her enthusiasm – which reminded me so much of my teenage days – made it impossible not to look up. The birthday girl was enthusiastically ripping the pretty gold paper which some other mother had carefully put together. 'Eye shadow and lip gloss! Thanks SO much. They're really wicked.'

I waited for the inevitable comment beside me. 'Make up! At their age!' My neighbour pursed her lips which, it goes without saying, didn't have a trace of lipstick. 'No wonder they grow up too fast. And just look at that girl's earrings not to mention her skirt-length. She might as well not bother wearing one.'

This woman was almost worse than the girls! I considered moving but the cowardly part inside me, was worried about being rude. Instead, I turned the page of my magazine and lost myself in the short story. It was so gripping that I almost missed my station.

'We're there,' shouted the girls.

'Lucky you,' said the woman grimly. 'They're getting off at your stop. If their mothers are there, you ought to give them a good piece of your mind.'

I muttered something non-committal and started to gather up my things.

'Come on, mum,' said the girl with hooped earrings and short skirt, tugging me by the sleeve. 'Or the train will leave with us still on it, and we'll miss the film.'

'Did she say "Mum"?' gasped the grey-haired lady. 'So they're yours?'

I glanced at my lovely daughter Julie who had made me promise – absolutely promise – not to embarrass her in front of her friends by telling them off or doing anything that might spoil her special day.

'Only one,' I said quickly, getting out of the carriage. As we all legged it down the platform in giggles, I thought I heard my former companion calling out. I couldn't hear clearly but it sounded something like 'Other people's children...'

7

First Person or Third?

When reading other people's short stories – an essential if you're going to get into the swing of it – you'll see that quite a lot are written in the first person.

There's a reason for this. In fact, at least two. The first is that many people find it easier to write in the first person. It comes easily to them because they can put themselves in the shoes of the main character and make that character like themselves.

The funny thing is that this works better in short stories than in novels. At least, it does in my opinion. The reason for this is that if you are going to write in the first person within a longer piece of fiction, it is more limiting. You have to stick to one viewpoint – your own – and this means you can't see or understand exactly what other people are doing.

You can of course, guess it. For example, John might think Julia is being very unfriendly. But he can't know for certain because he isn't Julia.

In a short story, however, you can get away with this more easily simply because it's shorter. There are fewer instances when you need to understand what other people are thinking or doing. It's as simple as that.

For instance, in the 'Laundry Basket' story which you will already have read, the heroine speaks in the first person. We don't get to meet the other characters although we do see them through their clothes. The story, however, is only 1,000 words long. If I'd had to keep this up for much longer, I might have floundered.

TWIST AND SHOUT

The second reason why writers like to write in the first person is because it allows them to give a twist to the story. You can do things with an 'I' that you can't do if you're describing someone else. For instance, you are not identifying yourself fully if you write in the first person whereas you do need to identify your characters if you're in the third person.

One of the most common examples of this is sex. I don't mean *that* kind of sex! I'm talking about gender. You could write a story in the first person in such a way that the reader might presume you're a woman – until you get to the end. Only then, do you reveal your true self.

I recently wrote a short story for *Woman's Weekly* in the first person about someone going to a health farm. From the description, it sounded very much as though the protagonist (that's the main person) was a woman. But when you get to the end, you discover something else. I won't spoil it for you because the story is at the end of this chapter.

In order to do this, however, you do have to sow seeds that mislead the reader. For instance, my character at the health farm is taking a much-needed break from the children which makes the reader think she's a woman.

The 'I' voice also allows you to get fully into the skin of your character. It's somehow easier to describe emotions and feelings and even write dialogue if you are imagining yourself in that role. As a result, your character might be more convincing.

EASY ON THE EAR

Remember why readers like short stories in magazines? It's because they need some rest and relaxation. Maybe that's why so many fiction editors buy stories in the first person. The reader can identify with the 'I' voice and will read on. However, that doesn't mean to say you should avoid the third person. On the contrary. Most fiction editors will say they want a mixture of both first and third person stories to choose from. So a story in the third person might end up on the desk of an editor who is looking exactly for that.

THE THIRD PERSON

The third person, however, can allow you to see and describe all your characters in depth. You can play around with them in a fuller way and this might open up the plot so you can do more with it. For example, in the multi-viewpoint stories I described in Chapter 5, the third person was essential. Instead of being inside their skin, I was up there in the gallery, manipulating them like puppets.

If you want to write in the third person but find it hard to get into the characters, try this invaluable tip which I've passed on to students over the years. Write one of the character's point of view in the first person. For example:

'I simply can't bring myself to ring him one more time. It's too embarrassing and he'll think I'm desperate.'

Try changing this to Julia's point of view.

> *'Julia simply couldn't bring herself to ring him one more time.*
> *It was too embarrassing and he'd think she was desperate.'*

Do you see how natural this sounds?

Read the following passage from a story I wrote in the third person and then turn it into the first person. See which one you feel most comfortable with.

> *Eve had always wanted to be Mary. But no one – least of all her*
> *– had ever considered herself to be Mary material. She was too*
> *plump without actually being fat. But more important, she just*
> *wasn't pretty enough. Carol, who sat next to her, had been*
> *Mary for their first nativity play at school and because she*
> *seemed so natural at it, she was Mary the year after that too.*
>
> *Eve had been a sheep.*
>
> *She could still remember how uncomfortable it had been,*
> *trapped in a blanket with cut-out eyes, crouched down on all*
> *fours and saying 'Baaa' at the right time.*
>
> *'Not a bad job, if I say it myself,' her mother had enthused,*
> *after the play. 'That blanket was a brainwave. But did you see*
> *the cow? Absolute disgrace in those lurid spotted tights. Mary*
> *was lovely, though. Such a pretty girl, Carol, isn't she?'*

THE STRONG AUTHOR'S VOICE

Sometimes the author's voice comes across so loudly and clearly, that it seems more intrusive than the ordinary third person. When

I say 'intrusive', this isn't a criticism. It's a matter of style. A loud author's voice can contribute a great deal to style and the voice of the story. It's rather like having a narrator who is telling the story while the characters act it on stage.

One example is the classic fairy tale opening: 'Once upon a time.' I personally don't write stories like this because I like to get into the character rather than seeing everyone from a distance but it might work for you.

TASTE IT AND SEE!

You might, as you read this, immediately home in on one of these methods and feel that is for you. But it's worth experimenting with all three; the first person; the third; and the overall author's voice.

There are other ways of describing these, by the way, with complicated phrases like third person subjective. But I don't think they help. In fact, they might take you straight back to bad memories of grammar lessons at school. So I've tried to make it as understandable as possible.

You'll get a chance to play around with this in the exercise below.

SUMMARY

- The first person allows you to write a story with a twist at the end.
- It might also help you describe a character more fully because you can identify with him or her.
- The third person gives you the scope to cover more characters and perhaps enlarge the plot. This is particularly useful for longer short stories.
- Try experimenting with different approaches.

◆ Write the first 200 words of a story in the first person.

◆ Now write the same story in the third person.

◆ Try writing it again with a strong author's voice.

This is a short story I wrote in the first person for *Woman's Weekly.*

—— Changing Rooms —— by Sophie King

ROOM 125. What a coincidence! Only five numbers more than the room I was in last year. Different hotel, of course. Different country, even. But nevertheless on the first floor.

Hotel room numbers are funny, aren't they? When you first check in, it usually takes a couple of days to remember it. Then, when you've been there a week or a fortnight, it becomes second nature; almost like your phone number. But the funny thing is that as soon as you go home again, you forget the number, don't you, because you don't need it any more.

Well, for some uncanny reason, I'm different. I seem to have this uncanny – and totally useless knack – of remembering my room number long after I've unpacked my holiday stuff and gone back to work. In fact, I can remember all the hotel room numbers I've ever been in.

ROOM 101. This was the first hotel room that Mike and I ever shared (we'd got a Special Offer through our local travel agent). It wasn't our first holiday together because we'd gone camping for the previous three years so I thought I knew Mike quite well. But it was a shock to find how forgetful he suddenly got when we reached Sardinia. If he went out on his own, he could never make his way back to the room, without checking the number at reception first.

In the old days, they used to put the number of the room on the key. But I suppose they have to be more careful now. Just as I should have been more careful with Mike.

ROOM 364. That was the room they put us in the following year. Rome, it was. Or was it Venice? That's the problem with me. Or at least, that's what Mike used to say. I remember the unimportant things but not the things that mattered. Come to think of it, it was Rome because I remember queuing for hours outside the Vatican museum. I'd wanted an ice cream to while away the wait but Mike said they were a ridiculous price.

It was quite a nice room although Mike complained about the air conditioning. 'It's always noisy,' I told him, 'in these kind of hotels.' But he complained so we were moved to . . .

ROOM 237. It was only for the remaining five days of our holiday and frankly, I didn't think it was worth it. Still, I always think there's a purpose in life for everything, especially as that's where I met Carlos. Carlos was the deputy hotel manager whom Mike had complained to. I could see in his face that he thought Mike was making a fuss but of course, he couldn't say so.

So when Mike went out again (threatening to complain to our travel agent back home) and Carlos offered me a complimentary drink in the bar to apologise for the noisy air conditioning, I found myself in . . .

ROOM 890. 'Wow! This is high up, isn't it?' I exclaimed as I looked out at the view. Way below me, like a tiny ant on the ground, I could see Mike on his mobile, head bent the way he did when he was having a serious conversation. Odd. I thought he said he was going out to change some money. Perhaps it was an urgent work call.

This room wasn't as nice as the others with its stark, single bed and bare floorboards instead of carpet. It was one of the staff rooms, Carlos explained but when he tried to give me a tour, I suddenly got cold feet. What was I doing here with a strange man? So that's how, the following year, I found myself in . . .

ROOM 5. You can see that I had to take a drop in my lifestyle. No more high-rise smart hotels now. Still, it was my choice, especially when I opened Mike's mobile phone bill on our return and discovered those calls hadn't been work-related at all. Funnily enough, it was almost a relief because it explained why we'd been one of those couples who never talk to each other on holiday but just lie on adjacent beds, with a bottle of suntan cream and a wide pit of silence between them.

In fact, I really liked Room 5. It was on the ground floor of a small Greek taverna with a pool that only took a few strokes to get from one side to the other. But it was clean with a nice double bed (which I didn't actually need) and there was a lovely pink plant clambering up the outside wall, which wafted its scent in through the window. Without Mike to worry about, I spent my time lying by the pool with a good book, soaking up the sun.

I liked it so much that the following year, I tried to go back. But it was full. So then I ended up with the girls in . . .

ROOM 77. I knew this was a good sign because '7' is my lucky number. So I wasn't very surprised when a smiley, tall dark stranger invited me to have a drink with him at the bar. I declined on account of the wedding ring on his left hand but it cheered me up. As Anna, the girl at our travel agents, kept telling me, holidays are a great place to meet people.

Maybe it was the girls that discouraged would-be suitors. I use the term 'girls' somewhat loosely because we're all over 35 and everyone else, apart from me, is married. But my best friend Fiona said she fancied a week in the sun while her other half was on a golfing holiday and somehow it snowballed. Still, it was fun and I came back with a great tan.

ROOM 323. There's no way I can afford two holidays a year but then something amazing happened! I actually won a competition. All I'd done was fill in a form at the local supermarket and suddenly, out of the blue, a letter arrived to say I'd won a holiday for two in Las Vegas. I could have asked Simon from work who'd taken me out a couple of times. But to be honest, there wasn't much of a spark. So I asked my sister.

I could hardly believe my luck when I walked into 323. There was a bed the size of my kitchen and a shower which was so big, I could almost have put a sofa in it. In fact, I was so bowled over that when I came back from the swimming pool that afternoon, I suddenly couldn't remember my room number. This had never happened to me before! And the more I thought about it, the more I couldn't remember. Was it 323 or 232 or 322 or...

There was only one thing for it. I'd have to go back to reception and explain my dilemma. Except that the lift didn't appear to be working and I couldn't find the stairs.

'Can I help you?' I swivelled round to find myself face to face with a tall, dark, Italian-looking stranger with the word 'Manager' affixed to his lapel.

'Carlos?'

He looked equally surprised. 'Julie? I mean, Mrs Greene?'

'Actually, 'I said, wrapping my towel around me and wishing I'd put on the beach wrap which my sister had pinched, 'I'm not married any more.'

'And I,' he said, puffing out his chest, 'have been promoted to this resort as manager.'

It was just at that precise moment that I heard the distinct sound of a lift bell (so it was working again!) and who should come round the corner but my sister

Annie. Carlos took one look at her and I suddenly realised it was time to go back to the sunbed. Alone. Which brings me back to.

ROOM 125 (AND 126). It was Will's idea. Will is Anna's boss at the travel agency and he'd been sent out to Cyprus to test out a new resort. So he suggested I went with him. It's been a good three years since my sister's wedding to Carlos and to be honest, it seemed like a good idea.

'Nice room,' I said, admiring the lovely double in 125.

'Do you think so?' he said, pulling me onto his knee. Perhaps I ought to explain something here. It turned out that Will had had other ideas when he'd instructed Anna to e-mail me with special holiday offers. Apparently, he'd fancied me from the minute I first stepped through the door of his travel agency, all those years ago. Isn't that romantic?

Room 126, which adjoined 125, was just as nice. Two rooms, I hear you asking? That's right. One for the twins and one for us. We both proved to be fast workers in order to make up for lost time. And if you can't quite see our room number, that's because it's hidden by the notice below.

PLEASE DO NOT DISTURB!

Beginnings and Endings

Pat Richardson, the fiction editor of *Best* magazine, says she looks for three things when someone sends in a short story. The first is the word count. The second is the beginning. And the third is the ending.

> *'I read the first three paragraphs first and then the final three paragraphs,' she told me. 'If I like them, I read what's in the middle.'*

It goes to show, doesn't it, how important it is to stick to the brief. First you have to get the word count right. *Best*'s guidelines stipulate a maximum of 1,200 and since most stories are then cut to 1,000 words, you can see that you can't exceed that maximum dose.

Then there's the beginning. You simply have to grab the reader from the first line. And then you have to provide a satisfactory ending at the bottom of the page.

GREAT BEGINNINGS

This is why I covered characterisation and plot before this chapter. Hopefully, you will now have learned how to 'draw' a character in words so they jump out from the page at the reader.

But how can we do this? Let's try the following ways.

Supposing, for example, you had a character whom you just couldn't ignore. Maybe it's someone who is acting in an eccentric manner. I once wrote about a girl who had a passion for hats. Everywhere she went, she bought some kind of a hat whether it was a beret or a boater or a felt cloche or whatever style took her fancy. You'll find out why when we get to the endings section.

Or maybe we have a character that has a problem we sympathise with. I once wrote a short story called 'Scattering Bert' about a woman who didn't know where to scatter her great uncle's ashes. It could have been macabre but it was written with humour that appeared on the first line.

We could also have a character who starts off with a rhetorical question. This can be a good way of drawing in the reader because you automatically answer it in your head. And then you're involved.

Or we could have two characters talking in a piece of dialogue that we just can't put down. For example:

'Did you see that? asked Annie excitedly.

'No.' Susie was on all fours, cleaning Mrs Morris's oven which had seen better days. She looked up and wiped her forehead with a dirty hand before realising what she'd just done. 'What?'

Immediately, we want to know what Annie saw and why it was so important. So we do what the writer wants us to do. We read on.

EXERCISE

- ◆ Can you think of any other ways in which you could make your character leap out at you from the first line?
- ◆ Make a list in your Ideas Book and keep it for the exercise at the end of this chapter.

USING THE PLOT AS A HOOK

In a way, the above example with Annie and Susie is both character *and* plot. We're interested in Annie and Susie because they seem to have quite a lot of energy. We also feel for Susie because we've often done dirty housework tasks and wiped our faces or done something which has left a mark.

But there's also a potentially interesting plot here, too. Annie has noticed something and like Susie, we want to know what.

I once wrote a short story about a woman who kept thinking she spotted celebrities in the street or in the shop. She became obsessed with it. The opening line was: 'I first saw Cliff Richard when I went into Top Shop.'

Well, it's different, isn't it? And that's what fiction editors want. They want something that's different enough to jump out of the page at them and which is nothing like all the other submissions they get sent every day.

Alternatively, you could start with a paragraph expressing a situation that many people will identify with. For example, in a recent *Take a Break Fiction Feast* story of mine, I wrote:

'I was sitting in the Italian restaurant where we always used to go and wondering where my lunch date was.'

Will he turn up? What is he like? Is there a twist? Hopefully, we read on to find out.

ENDINGS

That's all very well but, as Pat Richardson has proved, the pudding has got to live up to its expectations. It's no good wetting someone's taste buds if you're not going to deliver. Unfortunately, I've seen several students' work where they think the ending is funny or ties it all up but in fact, it does neither.

So how can you write an unforgettable ending? My advice is to make sure that something happens. Otherwise, the reader feels cheated. It might not necessarily be a piece of action. It could be a character's realisation or the dawning of a certain emotion. But either way, it has to mark the end of the line in a way that is hopefully not too obvious.

It also needs that feel good factor. Although there are some short stories that end with someone in a bit of a mess, there should be an overall feeling that everyone's got their just desserts.

This also depends on the kind of story you are writing (see the following chapters). If you are penning a twist in the tale story, you need a surprise at the end which really is going to be a shock or surprise for the reader.

If you're writing a tug-at-the-heart short story, you need to leave the reader glowing with all kinds of emotions and wishing she or he could come back for more. For example, in the restaurant story, we find out towards the end that the 'lunch date' is in fact the reader's son who reminds her so much of the husband she lost many years earlier.

Ending examples

Remember the story about the girl who was obsessed by hats? Half-way through, we find she is desperate for a hat for a wedding. But it's only when we get to the final paragraph, that we find she likes wearing hats because she's just finished a course of chemotherapy treatment.

This is only revealed at the wedding reception, when a nice young man asks her why she hasn't taken off her hat. When she does, she expects him to be shocked but he isn't. The suggestion is that they then walk off into the sunset together.

I recently wrote a short story about mystery voices – the game on the radio when listeners have to guess the voice. My character is certain she knows which one it is but at the end, she says the wrong one by mistake – and in fact, it's the correct answer.

Don't worry if you don't know what the ending is going to be in advance. Often, this doesn't come to the writer until half-way through. Sometimes, you really feel you have a good story there but can't think of an ending which really works. My advice is to put it away for a short time and allow yourself to think about it. As the days go by and you do other things, you're bound to get some ideas.

IN THE MIDDLE

Of course, the middle bit is just as important. You can have a great beginning and a stunning ending, but if the story in between doesn't work, it will end up in the rejection bin. Hopefully, I've given you enough guidelines already on plot and character for you to sustain the wow factor of the opening paragraph.

TITLES

Don't forget titles when thinking about your beginning and ending. Titles can be a great way of drawing in the reader, if they're unusual. For example, my story about the niece who had to find somewhere to bury her great uncle, was called 'Scattering Bert'. It's different, isn't it? And it's one reason why people hopefully read on.

Sometimes, you might not think of a good title until you get to the end. That's fine. But be prepared to be flexible. Some writers think they need to stick with the original because that's what they thought of in the first place. And of course, that's not true at all.

SUMMARY

- Short stories have to grab the reader from the first line. You have one chance to get a bite!

- To do this, think of something fresh and different. Pick up an idea and turn it round to see it in another light. Ask the 'What if...?' question.

- You don't need to have the end worked out before you begin. In fact, sometimes, it's better not to. You might get an even more interesting ending while you are writing.

- Make sure the bit in the middle lives up to the stunning beginning and ending.

◆ Study the beginnings and endings of at least five magazine stories.
◆ Now write the opening four paragraphs to a short story and then the final four paragraphs.
◆ Also write a plot outline for the whole story.

Below is a short story I wrote for *Woman's Weekly* which demonstrates the importance of beginnings and endings.

—— Scattering Bert ——
by Sophie King

At the funeral, everyone agreed that he'd had a good innings. Well, at 92, you can't stay around much longer, can you? That's what great uncle Bert used to say when I visited him in his old people's home, except that's not what he called it.

'A home for the young at heart,' he would say, his eyes twinkling as he knocked back the bottle of wine that I'd secreted in my handbag for visiting hours, along with yet another quiz book. Of course, he took care to see no one noticed. 'Pour it into the tea cup,' he would instruct me, grinning from ear to ear. 'That way they'll think it's Earl Grey.'

Perhaps it was the wine that did it. Or maybe the two wives that had lived – and predeceased him a long time ago. It could have been his infallible sense of humour that did the trick. But whatever his secret was, everyone agreed he should have bottled it.

'I can't believe he's gone,' said his best friend Jack who was a mere 20 years younger. 'We're going to really miss him on quiz night.'

That was another thing. Bert's head was a walking encyclopaedia. He knew every mountain in the world and all the capitals. He could list every ocean and sea besides giving a rundown of most prime ministers and presidents since 1906. He knew the names of every tree and taught me to take bark rubbings from silver birches because they were my favourite. But what he really excelled at, was asking everyone else questions to see if they knew the answers too.

Character-building, he would call it. 'Now Hilary,' he would say from as young as I could remember. 'What is the capital of Australia?' And I would rack my brains to come up with the right answer. But the wonderful thing about great-uncle Bert was that he didn't make you feel stupid if you didn't know. He would simply give you a way of remembering so that it stuck in your mind for later on. 'You can remember that Canberra is the capital of Australia, he would tell me, 'because the first bit sounds a bit like Kangaroo. Get it?'

As he got older, and as I did too, his questions became more complicated. Thank goodness it was my children's turn this time. 'If I set out from home at 8am in the morning and walked twenty miles to the east, which towns might I visit on the way,' he would ask my youngest daughter Joanna. Her face would screw up with confusion. 'I dunno,' she would say and Bert would tut, but not in an unkind way. 'I'm only trying to teach her some local geography,' he explained. 'The mind is like the body. It needs constant exercising.'

Thankfully, both great uncle Bert's body and mind were in great shape until almost the end. So much so that he had left his affairs in impeccable order. His small cottage had gone to me, his only surviving relative and his limited savings to the pub quiz team for beer money. There was only one outstanding matter which he hadn't resolved as Don, his solicitor (also a member of the quiz team) explained with a rather embarrassed look on his face.

'Bert left firm instructions that he was to be cremated,' he said. 'But he also said that you would have to work out where he wanted his ashes to be scattered.'

'That's ridiculous,' I spluttered. 'How on earth would I know?'

Don pointed to the relevant clause in great-uncle Bert's will. 'This is the final question for my great niece Hilary. She will know the answer when she finds it, as I am sure she will.'

I stared at Don in disbelief. 'But I don't. It could be anywhere. And what if I get it wrong?'

He squeezed my hand sympathetically (I've known Don since school days so that wasn't as familiar as it sounds). 'We could always argue he was of unsound mind and just pop him in the graveyard.'

'No.' I shook my head firmly. Great Uncle Bert had never been a churchgoer and besides, it would be an insult to his memory if I had said he was of unsound mind. Don nodded. 'I agree. I was just trying to be practical. Now Hilary, have a good think. What did Bert enjoy doing and would it be in the sort of place where he would want his ashes scattered?'

It would have been macabre, I thought, over the next few days, if it hadn't been for the fact that this was exactly the kind of joke that great uncle Bert would have enjoyed so much. It got the whole village going, including the pub quiz team, who were keen to come up with the right answer. Everyone agreed, much to the landlord's relief, that the Rose and Crown wouldn't be a practical option as the garden had now been converted into a car park. Bert wouldn't want to be there; he had walked everywhere and despised townies who relied on what he called their 'motors'.

'Don't even think of the pub,' he seemed to say in my head. 'I've had to give that sort of thing up, now.'

'What about his garden?' suggested my now grown-up daughter who had spent hours talking to great uncle Bert in his vegetable garden. (It explains why she is now a horticulturist, something which my great uncle was extremely proud of and took no small credit for.)

But I wasn't sure that he would want that either. Although he liked his garden, it wasn't his over-riding passion in life. 'Quite right,' great-uncle Bert seemed to say. 'From where I'm sitting, there's more to life than marrows, I can tell you. Come on Hilary, can't you guess where I want to be?'

Well I tried. I went through all the options but none of them seemed to provide the right setting for a scattering of ashes. Bert liked the mobile library but that was out of the question for obvious reasons. ('That reminds me,' he seemed to say. 'There are a couple of books on the hall table, that are well overdue now. Take them back for me, that's a good girl.') He also enjoyed playing bowls but the groundsman wasn't keen on having his turf moved around. During his latter years, great uncle Bert had taken up gliding but surely he wouldn't have wanted me to have scattered them from a great height? 'Who knows where they might land,' he seemed to mutter disapprovingly in my head.

This was getting ridiculous. Meanwhile, the said ashes were sitting in a blue and white china jar at Don's office. 'They can't stay there for ever,' I said when I popped in that morning to discuss the problem one more time. Honestly, I'd seen more of Don during the last month than I had done since my divorce – and that was years ago.

'They're no trouble to me,' said Don, making me a cup of coffee. 'Actually, I find them rather comforting. He was a wise old boy, your great uncle Bert. You know Hilary, you'll probably think I'm a bit mad but sometimes, when I'm sitting here at my desk trying to work something out, he seems to give me the answer. Take this property dispute I'm handling. Naturally, the details are confidential but last night, when I was looking at the papers again, the answer came to me, just like that. And it was in your uncle Bert's voice, too.'

I felt a great surge of relief. 'He's doing that to me too but it's probably just my imagination because I miss him so much. He always had the answers, didn't he? He even knew I shouldn't have married Dennis even though he didn't so much as say so. There was one particular day when we were sitting on the edge of the cricket pitch...'

I stopped. 'That's it! I gasped. 'I've got it. Of course! What did everyone say when Bert died?'

Don frowned. 'That we wouldn't win the quiz this year?'

'No!' I pulled him to his feet. 'That he'd had a good innings!'

Don's face began to clear. 'Didn't he play for the village cricket team when he was younger?'

'Yes. Come on. Let's go. He'll tell me if it's right when we get there.'

Slightly surprising for the middle of the week, there was a match in progress when we arrived. For a few moments, we stood and watched the white figures gracefully moving around the village green. But somehow I didn't get the blinding feeling I'd expected; hard as I tried, I just couldn't hear that inner voice from Bert that said, 'Yes this is where I want to be.'

'Good game isn't it?' said the man keeping the score. 'Sorry, I don't believe we've met. I'm the new rector of St Johns. Bill Williams.'

'And a keen cricketer, I see,' said Don thoughtfully.

'Absolutely.' He turned to me. 'You're Bert's niece, aren't you? I only knew Bert for a short time but he often used to turn up here during practice. We'd spend hours discussing cricket and God.'

I was astounded. 'But my great uncle hardly ever went to church. And without wanting to seem rude, I never remember him being that interested in God.'

'Ah,' said Bill smiling gently. 'But he was. He was just a bit scared of him.'

'Scared. Why?' asked Don.

'God is the one mystery in life that Bert couldn't quite get his head round. Not that any of us can, to be honest. But Bert didn't like that. He wanted to know everything he could about life; and he didn't like unanswered questions.'

That was true enough. But why had he never mentioned it to me?

'He wouldn't have wanted to have worried you,' said Bill simply as we walked past the cricketers. 'But he knew his time was almost up and I think, through our discussions, he was beginning to feel better prepared.'

By now, I realised we were standing in the graveyard. It's not a big one and the stones bore several of the same surnames on them, reflecting the families who had lived in the village during previous years. In the corner, was a silver birch tree, just like the one that Bert had taught me to take bark rubbing from.

'Here,' I said suddenly. 'This is where he wants to be.'

'Sure?' asked Don, putting a hand on my arm.

'Of course I'm sure,' said great uncle Bert in my head. 'Now go on. What are you waiting for?'

'Actually, there's just one more question,' said Don rather bashfully as Bill tactfully walked away. 'Only this time, I'm the one who's going to ask it. Hilary, I asked you before in the school playground all those years ago and you gave me the wrong answer then. So now I'm going to ask you again. Will you marry me?'

'Go on,' whispered Uncle Bert. 'You know the right answer.'

So I gave it to him.

Of course it was Yes. What a silly question...

9

Twist in the Tale Short Story

If you've done your market research properly by reading as many magazines as you can, you'll see that there are certain publications which regularly run what are known as twist in the tale stories.

Take a Break magazine is one example. This means that every week, the fiction editor is looking for a good, strong story in that genre. (Genre means 'type' of story for those of you who are just beginning.) In other words, it's a ready-made market. All you need to do is come up with the goods.

But what is a Twist in the Tale story? Basically, it's a story with an ending that takes the reader by surprise. The surprise needs to come as late as possible in the story. The longer you can spin it out, the better. Ideally, the twist should appear in the last paragraph or even the last line.

HOW CAN YOU MAKE IT HAPPEN?
The trick is to build up a picture slowly, during the story. A picture that sucks the reader into one way of thinking and then suddenly – without much warning – changes so that the reader sees something completely different.

If you've done it well, the reader will ask herself how that could happen. And that's where you'll have needed to have used all your skills as a writer. If the twist is so different that it's actually unbelievable, the reader will just mutter 'That couldn't really happen' and turn over the page, feeling very disgruntled and let down. Even worse, she might not bother reading anything of yours again. So it's essential that the twist could be seen as something that might really happen.

One way of achieving this is to plant clues throughout the story. This is known as foreshadowing. The crucial bit about this is that the clues mustn't seem too obvious. But at the same time, they have to be convincing enough so that when the reader gets to the end and is surprised by the twist, she can then go back and see the clues. Ideally, she'll then say to herself 'Why didn't I guess that earlier?'

An example of a 'twist' story

I recently wrote a short story for *Take a Break* about a couple who were going on a cruise (or so the reader was led to believe). The story 'talked' you through the different places they went to. But at the end, you find out that they didn't go on a cruise at all. They had just spent their holiday going on day trips.

When you looked back through the story, there were several clues. For instance, the young couple in question didn't have much money. The scene that made the reader think they were in France, actually showed them in a local art gallery which had an exhibition of French pictures. When the reader thought they were in Italy, they were actually having an Italian meal at the local restaurant. And so on.

The final twist came at the end when the couple did finally go somewhere – the local hospital. Only then do you find out why the couple couldn't really go away. Not because they were broke (although they didn't have many pennies to rub together) but because the girl was pregnant and about to have a baby. That's why they hadn't wanted to go far and why, instead, they'd plumped for day trips.

I thought of the idea because some friends of mine couldn't afford to go away, so instead they had a fantastic time doing things in their local area which they'd never had time to do before. The woman wasn't pregnant – that idea came to me while I was writing the story. I also thought of the cruise concept because it allowed me to suggest that they were in different countries rather than just one. This mean I could spin out the plot even more.

HAVE A GO!

Below is a list of foreshadowing clues and situations with a potential twist. Some are more likely to work than others. See which ones you think could convince a reader.

♦ Girl is sick. (At the end, you find out she's pregnant.)

♦ Kind-hearted, out-of-work girl is always giving money to the tramp on the street. (At the end, she discovers he's a newspaper reporter researching a piece and he gives her a job.)

♦ Man in the story is always getting lost. (At the end, he finds himself in the right place and meets the right woman).

♦ Girl meets man who loves her but not her cat. He's always sneezing when the cat is around. (At the end, we discover he's allergic to a new washing powder he started to use at about the time they began dating.)

In the above examples, the first is too obvious. Sickness is an obvious clue to pregnancy. However, you could say she had a queasy stomach after a curry.

The kind-hearted girl story might be convincing (in fact, it was the basis of one of my stories which was later published) because the emphasis is on the other person – the tramp – and not her own predicament. The foreshadowing clues might include the description of the tramp. For example, he could be wearing a smartish shirt which she presumed someone had given him.

The man who is always getting lost? Where's the story? Pathetic, isn't it?

Girl meets man who loves her and not her cat. It's all right but it's still a bit of a cop out. Having said that, I used something similar in a recent plot.

USING WORDS OR PLACES OR NAMES WHICH MIGHT HAVE DOUBLE MEANINGS

Some time ago, I read a short story in which a character was in a garden nursery and spotted the plant aloe vera. Now I can't quite remember the exact details and I've been unable to source the story. But I seem to recall that when the character said 'aloe vera' out loud, the woman next to him was startled because her name was Vera.

She thought he'd said 'Hello Vera'. And as a result, something happened.

In another short story I recall reading, a character in a crime short story, thinks she's got away with something wrong when she hides in a lorry going to Perth. However, it turns out to be Perth in Australia – she thought she was going to Scotland.

Another favourite double-meaning device is to give a character a name which might be male or female. It's not until you get to the end that you find out his or her true identity. I did this with my character 'Mel' in the story for the *Sunday Express* called 'Eating In'. My heroine kept popping next door to her neighbour to borrow cooking ingredients but it turned out that her neighbour Mel was a man who had something else to offer besides a pint of milk.

AVOIDING CLICHÉS

Some would-be writers seem to think they can get round this. For example, that person seemed to act in different ways because she had a twin. Or someone's money worries were solved when they won the lottery. Or the character got out of a sticky situation by waking up and finding it was all a dream. Or the character was really an animal.

Clichés are to be avoided at all costs! They are not original and fiction editors are not amused by them. Don't make the mistake of thinking 'This is only a magazine story so it won't matter'. Magazine fiction is a very professional market. Like publishers of novels, fictions editors expect high standards.

EXERCISE

Below, I have reproduced the beginning of a short story. Look carefully at it and see if you can spot any clues that might suggest a surprising ending. Now write the rest and include a twist in the tale ending that fits in with some of the foreshadowing.

THE SCHOOL TRIP
by Sophie King

Amanda glanced exasperatedly at the group of giggling schoolgirls as they waited to be checked into the Acropolis hotel. She hadn't wanted to go on this so-called educational trip to Greece in the first place but someone had to go with Anne, the department head. At any other time, she'd have jumped at a trip to Greece. But there was one big drawback. Zoe Eckersley was going too.

Of course Zoe wasn't her real name. Last year it had been Hayley and the year before that, Kylie. 16-year-old Zoe liked to change her name almost as often as she tried changing the uniform. In theory, this was a plain grey skirt, just above knee level with a cream blouse and a grey and blue jumper. But Zoe had the knack of making this combination into something completely different.

On the last day of term, when the girls were almost sick with excitement at the prospect of the Greek trip, Zoe's jumper appeared to have stretched, giving it the effect of a very short dress. The grey skirt was just about visible except that it looked more like a underslip hem, just below the said jumper. Someone (maybe Caz, Zoe's best friend) had written 'Watch Out Greek waiters' on her left arm in red felt tip and 'Here We Come' on the right.

To make matters worse, Anne had been sick throughout the journey and had had to go straight to her hotel bed, leaving Amanda to cope with eight over-excited teenagers from an all-girls school.

'I can't believe I'm doing this,' thought Amanda as she signed her motley crew in on the register and collected the room keys. In fact, she would have thought of an excuse if it hadn't been for Andy.

Amanda was at the age when she was almost ready to settle down. In theory, her boyfriend Andy, was also at an age when he should be feeling the same. At times, he said he did and they would sit on Amanda's sofa in her little rented flat, leafing happily through advertisements for houses which they couldn't quite yet afford. And at other times, he was unable to see her for days at an end because he needed his space. Which was why, at this very moment, he had booked a last minute holiday with some old college friends, leaving her free to volunteer for the dreaded school trip with Zoe Eckersley and co.

'Now look you lot,' Amanda warned them as they started to unpack their luggage.

SUMMARY

◆ Be on the lookout for situations which could be seen in two ways. These might be potential twist in the tales.

◆ Do the same for names.

◆ Make sure your twist really is a surprise.

◆ Do everything you can to ensure it's believable.

◆ When you've finished, go back to the beginning and plant foreshadowing clues -- but only if they won't give the game away.

The following short story was published in *Take A Break* and demonstrates the twist in the tale.

—— Holiday with a Difference ——
by Sophie King

It wasn't fair... Here we were, almost at the end of the summer, and we still hadn't gone on holiday.

'Are you sure you don't mind, love?' asked my husband.

I gave him a loving look across the travel pages of the Sunday supplement. 'Of course not.'

Well how could I tell him the truth? It wasn't Mike's fault he'd been made redundant at the beginning of the year.

That afternoon, Mike went shopping and came back with a pile of holiday brochures. 'We're going on a Mediterranean cruise!' he said excitedly, pulling me down on the sofa next to him.

Had the lack of sun gone to his head? But as I listened to his plan, it began to make sense so that night, we packed our suitcases. The following morning, we found ourselves in Paris, munching croissants in a corner café. 'Isn't this nice?' said Mike, reaching out for my hand. I nodded happily. 'Great coffee,' I murmured.

'Only the French can do it this way,' agreed my husband. 'Now how about visiting that impressionist exhibition?'

We spent the afternoon absorbing French culture: Renoir, Monet, you name it. By the end of the day, I was almost fluent. 'C'est magnifique,' I said to Mike as we made our way to le Baton Bleu for dinner.

'Absolutement,' he replied. 'But we can't be too late or we'll miss the boat.'

The following morning, was Venice. I'd never been before but I've always dreamed of being punted along the canal. I lay down next to my husband and trailed my fingers dreamily in the water as a tall, dark boatman punted us along.

The next stop was Athens. I'd always wanted to go to the famous son et lumière at sunset and here we were! I could hardly believe it. It was slightly chilly but that wasn't going to put us off. Besides, it was a good excuse to wear my new sea-mist blue mohair cardi, a second-hand charity shop find, that I'd bought specially for the holiday.

We were so busy enjoying the sights during the day, that we were too exhausted to enjoy much of the night life on board. But one evening, just before docking at Turkey, Mike persuaded me to do a turn on the dance floor. And as I rested my head on his shoulder, I knew that I was the luckiest woman in the world.

The final stop was Barcelona. Mike insisted on buying me a Spanish silk scarf even though we couldn't really afford it. We also had a mouthwatering paella at a lovely little restaurant in a cobbled square where Mike took even more photographs.

On the way back, we sat on the deck and sipped cold lemonade. It wasn't baking hot but it was warm enough for me to wear one of my summer tops and for Mike to be in shorts. 'This has been one of the best holidays we've ever had,' I said, looking up from my book.

'Hello, there,' said a voice from over the fence. 'Haven't seen you for a few days. Been away, have you?'

Mike and I giggled from the top of our decking platform that Mike had built earlier in the year. 'You could say that.'

Bert, our neighbour, looked at us suspiciously. 'You're not very brown. Where did you go?'

Mike shrugged. 'Oh, you know, all over the place. France, Spain, Greece, Turkey.'

Bert frowned over his rhubarb sticks. 'A week's cruise? You packed a lot in.'

'That's true,' I said. 'But actually, it wasn't an ordinary kind of cruise.'

'No,' added Mike. 'It was a magic cruise. We couldn't afford a holiday so we had days out and pretended we were abroad. We imagined that we were going to Paris and had croissants at that new café down the road. Afterwards, we went to the new impressionist exhibition in town. For Italy, we visited Oxford for the day and hired a punt (with someone to row) us down the river. We even packed a suitcase first of all, to get us in the mood.'

'For Athens, we went to a musical soirée in Bath,' I chipped in. 'We took a fantastic picnic with feta cheese that we got from M&S. And for Turkey, we tried out one of those Turkish baths not far from here. In the evening, we danced around the lounge and pretended it was the ship's ballroom.'

'We didn't have any airport delays and we didn't have to bother with foreign currency,' added Mike. 'But the best thing was coming back to our own bed at night, instead of a lumpy mattress that sank in the middle like the one we had last year in Corfu.'

Bert nodded. 'I can see that all right. Don't hold with going away myself. I went to Weston-Super-Mare twenty years ago and I hated it.'

'You ought to try Barcelona,' I said, with a naughty smile. 'That was our last port of call yesterday. We visited a Spanish church in London and Mike bought me a real Spanish scarf from a stall in Oxford Street. In the evening, we found a Spanish restaurant and had a great paella although I must say, it's given me a bit of a funny tummy this morning. I hope it wasn't the shrimps.'

They both looked at me in alarm. 'Are you sure you're all right, love?' asked Bert. 'You need to take it easy at this stage, you know.'

'I think so. Whoops, maybe not.' I looked at Mike in alarm. 'That was definitely a twinge . . .'

And that was the other reason we couldn't go on holiday. I still had four weeks to go but as the doctor had said, it was probably best not to travel too far in my condition. Our beautiful baby girl was born that night. And as I held her in my arms, with Mike close to me on the hospital bed, I felt as though I had made a momentous journey in life. We'd been waiting, you see, a very long time for this baby – another reason for not taking any chances.

'Everything seems fine to me,' said the young doctor who was making routine checks. 'In fact, I can probably discharge you before too long.'

Mike and I smiled at each other. We both knew exactly what the other was thinking.

'I can't wait to get back,' I said.

'I agree,' said Mike, kissing the top of my head.

When you've gone as far as we have, there really is no place like home.

10

How to Write Feel-Good Stories or Tug-at-the-Heart Tales

Twist in the tale stories are great fun to do – providing you can think of a good plot. But not everyone can. What you can do, however (and I'm willing to take a bet on this) is think of a situation or person that makes you feel warm and good inside.

This, in itself, can be an essential part of the plot. How many times have you got to the end of a short story and thought 'Well, nothing much happened. But I still enjoyed it. It makes me feel all right about the world.'

And that's what it's all about. Most stories for magazines have one aim: to entertain and make people feel relaxed. If you can achieve that with a tug-at-the-heartstrings tale, you're there.

BUT WHAT ABOUT THE PLOT?
Of course, you still need a plot. But if you did the tree diagram (see Chapter 2) with a tug-at-the-heartstrings story, you might not find so many branches. This is because there might not be so much action.

But – and this is the big but – if you can still entertain and twang our feelings with enough emotion, this will make up for it.

On the other hand, you still need something to happen. Your characters still need to be strong and convincing. And they still need a problem to solve. It's just that you might choose to do this through using feelings rather than actions.

HOW DO YOU GO ABOUT IT?

There are all kinds of examples, aren't there, of situations that have that feel-good flavour?

- ◆ Christmas.
- ◆ Meeting up with someone after a long time.
- ◆ Finally getting pregnant.
- ◆ Passing an exam.
- ◆ Helping an elderly neighbour to dig his garden.

Feeling warm already? Great. That's what we want. Or is it? We need something to happen. Christmas is all very well with its present opening and big family lunch. But if that's all there is to it, where's the story?

Actually, it's lurking right there. Each one of those situations can be inverted or changed around to make a plot. After all, Christmas isn't always a good time for everyone, especially if someone is on their own or wants to be with someone else.

Meeting up with someone after a long time might be a situation you'd rather avoid if you didn't want to see that person. Getting pregnant could be a problem rather than a joy. Passing an exam might mean you have to move departments in the office. And while we're about it, suppose your elderly neighbour tripped over the garden fork and blamed you, even though you were only trying to help? Whoops! How do you get out of that one? This is where your writer's skill comes in.

GETTING OURSELVES OUT OF A HOLE

Let's take the Christmas theme. I once wrote a short story in which the heroine – a middle aged woman – is about to decorate the Christmas tree. As she unwraps each ornament, she is reminded of the time she bought it and this triggered off memories about her children who had now grown up.

The story behind the ornaments also told us a little about her own situation. For example, she remembers one set of coloured glass balls very clearly because her husband had brought them back from a business trip just before she discovered he'd been having an affair.

She also finds, while unwrapping the objects, that there's a crack in one of the balls. The crack gets her thinking. Should she, all those years ago, have mended the crack in her marriage just as the ball had been mended with glue?

The story continues with more memories centred around each object. You'll see that nothing dramatic has happened in terms of action. She hasn't fallen over the tree. A tall, dark, handsome stranger hasn't rung. She hasn't decided to leave it all and go to Spain for the week. So far, the story has relied on emotion.

But it's an emotion that hopefully, lots of us will recognise. Emotion from when her children were little and used to listen out for Father Christmas. Emotion from when she and her husband had been happy. And it tugs at our heart strings because we want it to be all right again.

Adding some action

And then something does happen. There's a ring at the front door but it's not the tall, dark, handsome stranger. It's her grandson whom she's looking after for the day. And again, we get more emotion. Our heroine might feel sadness for the past but there's a brand new future here, and he's jumping around on the sofa just as her children had done when they were small.

And then (the branches on the tree diagram are flourishing now), there's another knock on the door. It's our heroine's ex-husband who is calling round with presents for the children. And as they sit and chat over coffee because this was, after all, quite an amicable divorce, our heroine and her ex suddenly begin to wonder if it's not too late after all to mend those cracks.

I hope you're beginning to feel the 'ooh' or 'spine tingling' factor here. If we hadn't had all the emotional 'stations' before, this ride might have seemed too twee. But in fact, it could happen in real life. Couples do get back together and although it might be difficult, we don't have to deal with this now because it's a short story and not a novel.

The difficulties in getting back after a break, could be another short story altogether or a much longer piece. And in a way, that's one of the beauties of a short story. You can hint at something, rather like an artist might do a pen sketch before painting the bigger picture. And you can get away with something that might be harder in a longer piece.

MIX AND MATCH

Sometimes you can have a combination of a story with a twist plus lots of emotion. I once wrote a story about a woman who was looking after her grandson for the first time. She had him for the whole day while her daughter was with a friend and she was understandably nervous. Those of you reading this with grandchildren of your own, are possibly nodding your heads. After all, it's easy to get out of practice, isn't it?

I'm not a grandmother yet (at the time of writing, anyway!) but my children are almost grown up and I can imagine how nervous I would feel if someone put a newborn baby into my arms! So already, we've hit the 'Yes I recognise that' feeling which we talked about in Chapter 2.

My grandmother heroine also has problems putting up the brand new pushchair. The design is much more complicated than it was in her day and we understand that too, don't we? The pushchairs on the market nowadays look more like a cross between an aeroplane and car. You have to twiddle and fiddle certain knobs and it's not easy if you're holding a baby in one arm at the same time.

So far then, we've engaged with our heroine when it comes to emotions. She takes her grandson to feed the ducks and that reminds her of taking her daughter when she was a toddler. If you drew your tree diagram of action, there wouldn't be many branches at this stage.

Bringing in a twist

But then something happens. We learn through internal dialogue that the grandmother has a special reason to be nervous. She actually didn't bring up her own daughter when the latter was a baby. Why? Because she adopted her daughter when she was a toddler. Which explains why she isn't very good at all this baby stuff. She's never done it before. Just like a new mother.

So there's the twist which comes on top of lots of emotional layers. It's certainly another way to do it, isn't it?

SUMMARY

- Short stories don't have to be based on a scintillating plot. They can get their 'wow' factor from showing emotion.
- It needs to be an emotion which lots of us can understand.
- If you're stuck, think of situations or places or people which have meant a lot to you.
- Make sure you still have a plot.
- Try mixing and matching twists and emotions.

EXERCISE

Write a list of emotional situations which have happened to you or people you know. Here are a few to start you off:

- Losing something.
- Starting a new job.
- Going on a blind date.

Write down a list of emotions next to each topic. For example, with 'blind date', you could write:

- ◆ Nervous
- ◆ Clock watching
- ◆ Not sure what to wear
- ◆ Feeling sick

Now write down the beginning of a plot. Perhaps the heroine loses the bit of paper which says where she's meant to be meeting her blind date. What should she do?

If you can't think of something, start writing. Focus on the emotions. Our heroine has a blind date with a friend of a friend. She spends ages rifling through the wardrobe for a dress she wants to wear but can't find it. Then she suddenly remembers she's left it at the dry cleaners which shuts in precisely five minutes. If she dashes, she might just make it.

The above is a paragraph which just occurred to me as I was writing the first part of the exercise, probably because I need to pick up something from the dry cleaners myself. But supposing our heroine dashes to the shop and finds it has just closed. But the lights are still on, showing that the owner is still there, locking up. She presses the bell and the owner reluctantly comes to the door. Except that it's not the owner. It's the owner's son because his mother is on holiday. She explains the situation and they take one look at each other and . . .

Up to you to finish this one off!

Alternatively, you could write your own tug-at-the-heartstring story, taking into account all the points we've mentioned.

The following story was published in *Woman's Weekly* and demonstrates the tug-at-the-heartstring angle.

—— Decorating the Christmas Tree ——
by Sophie King

It was dark in the understairs cupboard but my hands knew what they were looking for. Every year, I put it back in the same place, right at the back, wedged behind the pile of family photograph albums.

There it was. A large cardboard box which had, over the course of time, become slightly battered but nevertheless, still served its purpose. I was reluctant to replace it; the box itself had become as historically important to me, as had the contents.

Careful not to drop it, I crawled back on my knees back into the hall. In the light, the box seemed as I always remembered it yet also different – as though it too, like me, had changed in the previous year during which we hadn't seen each other. Christmas Decorations! My mother's handwriting on the top, in her distinctive feminine loopy style complete with exclamation mark, always gave me a jolt. It still strikes me as weird that handwriting can long outlive someone who has died and almost fool the people who are left behind, that the deceased is still there.

It would have been sensible to have waited until carrying the box into the sitting room where the tree was waiting. But my fingers refused to be patient and I found myself opening it up and unwrapping one of the tissue-wrapped figures excitedly, just as I remembered doing as a child. Decorating the tree had been a tradition which I always did with my mother. 'Look Annie!' she would say excitedly. 'This little rabbit bell was given to me by my grandmother when I was your age.'

A rabbit bell? I can still recall my curiosity when I took from her a small red china bell with rabbit ears on the side and a painted face on the front. When I rang it, the excitement of Christmas rang through me with its tinkly peal and I half-expected Father Christmas to come charging in through the front door (which my mother always adorned with a garland made from sprigs of garden holly).

Now, ironically, it was the rabbit bell I was unwrapping now. I held it up wonderingly. Of course it was silent now. I thought back to the Christmas many years ago when my eldest son had had an argument with his younger brother. 'I want to decorate the tree,' Richard had yelled. 'No, I want to do it first,' Bruce had retorted. Before I could stop them, they had started fighting over the poor little rabbit bell.

'Stop it both of you!' I had cried, launching myself in between them. Too late. As I wrenched the bell from their grip, there was the sound of a crack. 'You've broken it,' I had sobbed. And as I cried, with my then young sons looking on in horror (I usually saved my tears for after bedtime), I wept bitterly for my mother who had died only that year and who would never again be there to decorate the tree or watch her grandchildren growing up.

My husband Mike had glued the bell together for me but the stick that chimed was past saving. Now, all these years later, I gently stroked the glue line, marvelling that something which had been broken so long ago, could still be in one piece.

I put the rabbit bell back and took the box into the sitting room. Sitting cross-legged (tricky now arthritis has set in), I unwrapped the next piece. Of course! The set of silver balls which my husband Mike had bought in China during a business trip. Mike always used to be on business trips. He only just got back in time from the China one when our daughter was born a week before Christmas; five years after our family was 'complete'. Mike invariably bought me nice presents back from these trips abroad; the more expensive they were, the more I knew he'd been enjoying himself. So I was actually quite pleased to have this fairly modest gift of six silver balls. 'I thought they'd be nice for the tree,' he said while decorating it with the boys. 'No, you sit down, Annie. You ought to rest.'

That was the only year I didn't dress the tree. A new baby meant there wasn't much time for that sort of thing especially as both boys hated their sister on sight. So much so that they actually stamped on one of the silver balls in anger. They also broke another when wrapping them up again which explained why there were only four balls now. Still, as Christmas casualties go, it wasn't that much of a disaster. I hung them in symmetrical fashion half-way up.

What was this? I unwrapped an odd looking shape from the tissue paper. Of course. How could I have forgotten? A gold-coloured paper star that Katy had made when she was at primary school. Gently, I put it on a branch towards the top, remembering how she had proudly brought it back, grinning toothily as I oohed and aahed over it. 'Show it to daddy,' she'd demanded.

Well, I would have done if he'd been there. But Mike was away on another 'business trip' except that by then, we both knew what he really meant. 'Why don't you just leave him?' demanded Richard who at the age of 16 was old enough to know what was going on. But it wasn't so easy in those days. I hadn't worked for years so how would we manage financially? It's different for women now and I half-envy them for their independence. Besides, I still loved him . . .

Every Christmas, it had been a tradition to buy something new for the tree, just as my mother had. It gave the decorations a sense of history. I could match each piece with memories of what had happened that year. But the following December, we made do with what we had. Mike had taken matters into his own hands; that Christmas it was just the children and I with a rather small turkey. But we still decorated the tree and, to my surprise, I found I enjoyed it far more than in previous years when I'd always had half an ear open for the click of the key in the lock and the inevitable excuses which I had pretended to believe.

The children had seemed more relaxed too. In fact, they didn't fight as much as usual. 'Here, Katy, you put the tinsel on that branch there,' instructed Bruce. Richard was already disentangling the fairylights. Usually, there was always one bulb which didn't work and which consequently messed up the complete circuit. But this year, for once, they all worked. 'That's beautiful!' cried Katy in delight. The boys hugged me. 'It's going to be all right, mum,' said Bruce. 'We just need to work together as a team.'

The following Christmas, Richard took charge of the tree tradition. 'I'm the man of the house now,' he said after driving back with a no-drop, five footer in the boot of his car. Katy had made a new angel. She was good at sewing – not like her mother – and had stitched a beautiful satin white skirt around a small doll and made a wand out of tinsel and a matchstick. Even in those days, I could tell she was going to be an artist. 'Make a wish, mum,' she'd demanded. So I did. It wasn't what they would have expected (of course I didn't tell them). It wasn't what I expected to wish for either (but the words came into my head). And then I forgot about it.

The years went by. Richard went to work rather than college and Bruce went to college instead of work as I had expected. The house felt so empty that I suggested to Katy that perhaps we ought to get an artificial tree instead of a real one as it would be 'less bother'.

'Less bother?' my daughter had exclaimed in horror. 'How could you, mum? We've always had the real thing. Even the year dad went.'

It was the first time she'd mentioned it but when I tried to talk about it, she clammed up again. By the time Katy went to art school, we had got through two more pairs of fairy lights (why don't they last long?) and I had actually found myself a job as a classroom assistant. It was right up my street and when I had to help my little class make decorations for their Christmas trees at home, I was in my element.

'Look,' I explained to a group of starry-eyed seven year olds who were high with pre-Christmas excitement. 'This is how you make dough stars.' I'd genned up of course, on the internet, with a recipe for dough shapes and to my delight, they turned out rather nicely even if I say so myself. The look on the children's faces reminded me poignantly of my own little brood at that age. Then I remembered the arguments and couldn't help thinking that actually it was much easier now they were grown up . . .

'You bought something new for the Christmas tree,' exclaimed Katy, holding up my dough tree when she came back for the Christmas holidays last year with her boyfriend. Richard was coming too with his wife and three year old Joe although Bruce was still in Australia (he'd promised to phone on Christmas Eve). I could see she was pleased I'd resumed my old tradition of getting a new decoration every year. 'I made it with my class. Do you like it?'

'I do.' Katy gave me a warm hug. 'I love Christmas, mum. You always make it so wonderful.'

Last year was also the first time that Joe helped me decorate the tree. 'It's a special occasion,' I whispered into his ear as we kneeled by the tree, unwrapping the decorations. 'That's right. Hang the rabbit bell there. But be careful, love. It's very very old.'

'Why doesn't it ring if it's a bell?' asked Richard's wife.

'It's a bit of a long story,' said Richard amidst the laughter. 'And as it doesn't reflect very well on me, we won't go there if you don't mind!'

This year, all the children were going to be here although of course they weren't children any more. Bruce was finally back from his travels. And Katy was coming with a new boyfriend (I knew the last one wasn't right after he accidentally stepped on a silver ball, leaving only three). Richard and his wife were expecting another baby. And Joe was apparently itching to decorate the tree with granny.

It was time now to unwrap the final piece of tissue paper. But it wasn't in the box. It was in the bottom kitchen drawer where I had hidden it after it had arrived in the post a few weeks ago, along with a note. I drew out the red papier mâché heart and wondered what to do with it. At first, I'd ignored it. At my age, I'd long stopped expecting true love to arrive. Besides, whatever Mike's faults, I found it difficult to think of being with anyone else.

But now, here was my chance.

As if on cue, the doorbell rang. Still holding the heart, I went to open it. Mike stood on the doorstep; older and greyer than when I had last seen him but in another way, just the same.

'Thanks for letting me come,' he said, bending briefly down to kiss my cheek.

I stood back to examine him more carefully. We'd both learned a lot over the years, Mike and I, especially since we'd started meeting every now and then. I had learned that people can genuinely change. And he'd learned that the grass isn't always greener under someone else's Christmas tree.

'I'm just doing the decorations,' I said casually. 'Do you want to help?'

Together we walked across to the small spruce that I had bought that week from the garden centre. 'I can't really start until Joe arrives,' I said. 'I promised. He'll be here any minute.'

Mike nodded. 'A promise is a promise,' he agreed.

I paused, thinking of the wish that Katy had made me make over the angel, all those years ago.

'On the other hand,' I added, 'perhaps he wouldn't mind if we just hung one piece.'

We both looked at the red rabbit bell with its crack down the side. It might have lost its chime but it was still beautiful to me because of the history it represented. Just like a marriage that had once seemed fatally flawed. Gently, Mike took my hand and together, we hung the rabbit bell on the top branch of the tree. And then we hung the red heart next to it.

'To future Christmases,' he said softly.

As the doorbell rang, I could hear our grandson jumping excitedly up and down on the doorstep. And I knew that this year, our tree was going to look its very, very best.

$$11$$

How to Write Ghost and Mystery Stories

I have to confess here that this is not one of my specialist areas. I think it's because I write best about what I know. And I have never – or so I believe – seen a ghost.

I have, however, felt a distinct chill and premonition at times. That feeling when the hairs at the back of your neck stand up. Or when you go into a room that seems much colder than the rest of the house. Or hearing footsteps above when you know there isn't anyone else in the house. So if I had to write a ghost story, those are the kind of emotions I would tap into.

Writers of ghost stories tell me that they fell into this genre almost by accident. 'I entered a competition where the ghost had to be the main character,' said a writer who prefers to remain anonymous because she specialises in romance and doesn't want her readers to get confused. 'Because it had a theme everyone had to stick to – it was the Unexpected Ghost at Christmas – it made it easier because I had a tight brief.'

HOW TO GET STARTED
I think there are two messages in the above quote. The first is that you don't know if you can write a certain kind of short story until you start. And the second is that it can help, with a subject that might not be your first choice, to have a tight brief. You can do

this by using a ghostly theme from a competition, even if you don't enter it, as inspiration.

Or you can set yourself a brief by pretending you're giving homework to someone else. Here are some examples. Write a short story or plot outline about:

◆ a ghost who moves in next door;
◆ a cat that comes back from the dead;
◆ a ghost who's scared of people;
◆ someone who doesn't believe in ghosts.

You may well find when starting, that your chosen topic doesn't inspire you. That's fine. Perhaps by starting, you might have thought of something else instead. For example, the ghost that was scared of people might begin with the ghost as the main character. But then, if it was me, I'd change it to a young girl moving into her first flat in a converted Victorian house. She keeps hearing footsteps in the next room but every time she goes in, they run away.

She then has a series of dates with a boyfriend whom the ghost disapproves of (although we don't know that yet). Every time he comes to dinner, the ghost makes even more noise. This continues through various boyfriends until the girl finally meets someone the ghost approves of. And then the noises stop. As a final twist, it turns out that the approved boyfriend used to live near this house as a child. He had a childhood friend here who died many years ago...

Isn't it interesting how stories can turn out? I didn't think of this idea when I began exploring the theme of ghosts who were scared of people. And in the end, it wasn't about that at all, was it? So the trick – or part of it – is to start writing and then let your imagination take over. In fact, I think I'll start writing that story when I've finished this chapter!

USING REAL-LIFE EXPERIENCES

If you've had experience of ghosts or ghostly feelings in real life, use them in your fiction. When my children were younger, we lived in a remote farmhouse. I actually asked if it was haunted when we moved in and was assured it wasn't. But my children kept saying they saw a blue light in the corner of my bedroom if they came in during the night. I spent many evenings there alone and never felt threatened or scared.

But after we moved, the new people rang to say their young daughter reported being lifted over the stair gate by a 'blue lady'. We contacted the people we had bought from and they confessed that it was haunted by a woman in blue who had once been 'disappointed in love'.

Now I have to say that this idea has haunted me every since. But if I did use it in a short story, it would need to be a long short story because it's not something that could be wrapped up and solved in 800 words.

On the other hand, I do have a couple of other real-lifes up my sleeve. Once, when digging the garden, I found a metal heart-shaped tin. It looked as though it should have a lid but it was missing. Who threw it into the vegetable patch (which is where I found it)? Was it a girl after a lover's tiff? Had someone else taken it from her?

I'm going to leave that one up to you. As an early exercise, you could write down two or three ideas on what you could do with the heart tin story. It doesn't have to have a ghost in it but it needs to have some kind of mystery.

Using poetic licence

You could also use your poetic licence to shape something from an incident which was potentially spooky even if it wasn't. A few months ago, my teenage daughter had some friends to stay overnight. Suddenly, at about 3am, I was woken suddenly by someone coming in through my bedroom door and heading for my ensuite. I called you 'Who are you?' and he answered 'James'. He used my bathroom and then went out of my room, leaving me speechless and terrified in bed.

It turned out that he had been sleep walking but when I recounted this tale to a psychologist friend afterwards, he said: 'Wouldn't it have been spooky if, after you'd asked him who he was, he'd turned round and said "Who are you?"'

That made me think. Supposing I had got up and seen that everything in 'my' bedroom had gone and that someone else's things were there instead? Somehow, I had been moved into someone else's world even though it was my bedroom. Now that might be an interesting one, mightn't it?

MORE INSPIRATION

Use stories from newspapers and magazines to give yourself ideas.

When I had just got to the end of this chapter, I happened to read a snippet in a tabloid newspaper about a librarian who was very surprised when he heard the lavatory flushing after he'd locked up the library for the night. This continued every evening until at last he reported it. The authorities vouched that he was telling to the truth but there was nothing in the article to say what would happen next. Would an exorcist be called in? Would they just leave the ghostly reader to his own devices? Surely there's a story here, waiting to be written . . .

CHARACTERISATION

That's right! Ghosts have characters too. The funny thing is that although we're usually scared of ghosts, many stories depict them as being friendly when you get to know them. Of course, this isn't always true, especially in longer fiction when they can be threatening and add to the air of tension.

But in a short story, in my opinion, a ghost needs to be friendly. This is because you haven't got room to expand the situation into one where the ghost is malicious or unkind. You have anything between 800 and 1,800 words to make it all right in the end and a scary ghost might not be the right medium (if you'll excuse the pun).

You could possibly have a difficult ghost that brings two people together or makes something nice happen. But I've never seen a nasty ghost in a short story and I think there's a reason for it.

Bear in mind that ghosts can also have a sense of humour, just like us. In fact, humour and comedy in a mystery story can be light relief and make it stand out from others, especially in a competition. Readers might be grateful for an opportunity to have a laugh and ease the tension.

IT'S A MYSTERY

Mystery stories don't have to be ghost stories – although they can be. Again, I think the best mysteries come from real life. If you don't have a mysterious experience yourself, listen to other people. Or ask someone about the most mysterious thing that happened to them. It might give you an idea or two.

The television and radio can also be good sources for mystery ideas. The other day, I heard someone phoning in to talk about an experience they'd had recently. It was a woman who had been driving along a strange country road when she saw the most beautiful house on the left-hand side, all lit up. It was so lovely that when she stopped at the pub for a bite to eat, a little further on, she asked who lived there.

'What house?' asked the publican, confused.

One of the regulars, who'd lived in the village all his life, overheard the conversation. 'Ah,' he said. 'You're one of the lucky ones.'

What did he mean?

Apparently, only a few people ever see this house which burned down many years ago. But every now and then, it appeared to people who are particularly sensitive . . .

Sends shivers down your spine, doesn't it?

SUMMARY

◆ Try your hand at a ghost or mystery story. You might not think it's your cup of tea but you could be pleasantly surprised. If it doesn't work, you know it's not for you.

◆ Look out for ghost and mystery competitions. They might give you ideas.

◆ Think of ghostly or mystery situations which you've experienced in real life. Ask others if they've had any, too.

◆ Use them as a base and see what you come up with.

◆ Remember your limitations with a short story. It all needs to be tied up neatly at the end. Editors don't like endings which are vague.

◆ Remember that ghostly and mysterious stories can have humour.

EXERCISE

Write a ghost story based on your own experiences of something mysterious. If you don't have any, interview someone who has. The length can be anything between 1,200 and 2,000 words.

(12)

Seasonal Stories

One of the biggest mistakes that short story writers make, is to suddenly realise that Christmas or Valentine's Day or another big day in the year is about two months away or maybe less. 'Great,' they think. 'I'll send in a story that's relevant to that day.'

Well, it might be relevant to that day but it might not be right for that year! Most fiction editors have chosen a story for a special date or time well in advance. So the trick is for you to beat everyone else and send in your story several months in advance.

Providing it's a story with a difference, that will stand out from the others, you stand a good chance of getting in there. The fiction editor will pounce on a story like this with a sigh of relief and think 'There's a week I won't need to worry about now.'

I'VE GOT A GREAT IDEA

The trick, however, is not just timing. It's also, as I've briefly said, the kind of story you put forward. The downside to seasonal stories is that you need to think of something very different. And when a fiction editor has seen several years' worth of Valentine stories about couples who make up or break up, he or she wants something different.

So how do you do it? I've mentioned before that I teach all my creative writing students to pick up an idea and look at it from underneath, round the sides and every which way except the normal one. Let's think about New Year, for instance. Recently, I knew that a features editor was looking for a New Year story and even though I am one of her regulars, I knew I needed to find something different.

Finding a different point of view

So I asked myself what people usually do on New Year. They go to a party or if they're on their own, they spend it with a bottle of wine and a DVD. (I've had a few of those myself, recently.) But what if my heroine was a party girl who, for some reason, couldn't go out. Why couldn't she? What was preventing her? A dose of chickenpox? A broken leg? All too obvious. But what if she was stuck in a lift?

Possible. But why would she be in a lift if she was at a party? Because the party was being held in a swanky hotel. And what was she doing in a lift at 20 minutes to midnight? Because she'd gone to the party and something – or someone – had made her run out to escape. OK. Maybe an ex-boyfriend whom she wanted to avoid. But what would she do in the lift? Nothing. And that's what would give her time to think instead of rushing round as she usually did.

We're getting somewhere now. But what would help her in the lift and, more importantly, move the plot along so we didn't all get bored to tears? Well, besides taking us through her life story in 800 words, she could also be comforted by the voice of the lift repair man as he spoke to her through the tannoy in the lift.

And when he finally got her out (past midnight), she realises that although the lift man isn't her usual sort, there was something about his voice that made the New Year look a lot more promising than it had before.

CHANGE SEX!

Another way of making your season story stand out is to change the sex of the character. Now I'm not advocating a sex change here as that would definitely be a longer plot. What I'm suggesting is that you write the story in the first person in such a way that the reader thinks it's a woman but it's really a man – or vice versa.

We've covered this twist idea before but it can be used very effectively in seasonal stories. Take a story I wrote about Mother's Day. It's in the first person and in the first quarter of the story, where the 'heroine' is looking through past Mother's Day cards with nostalgia tinged with sadness, you fear the child in question is dead.

Then the little girl suddenly arrives back from nursery with her childminder Teresa. Our heroine is worried because the childminder hands her two cards. One is a Mother's Day card and the other is an envelope. She fears the envelope contains the childminder's resignation and is scared because she doesn't know how she'd manage without her. It is, after all, very tough being a single parent.

Revealing the twist

And then, three quarters of the way through, we find the little girl calling our heroine 'Daddy'. Our main character is in fact the father and it's the mother who had died two years ago, leaving the father feeling bereft. But then he opens the childminder's envelope and finds it contains two tickets for the theatre. And suddenly, he sees Teresa in a different light.

When you look back over the story, you can see clues that the mother is really the father. But it's not obvious at the time. Because it's written in the first person, I didn't have to use 'he said'.

I thought of the idea because certain occasions in the year are very difficult for people to cope with. A single parent might find Christmas tough if their children are with their former partners. Mother's Day can be agonising for anyone without a mother and the same goes for Father's Day. It's worth bearing this in mind as a starting point for finding a story which might provide hope for people in these situations and who are tired of reading stories about conventional lives.

OCCASIONS YOU MIGHT NOT HAVE THOUGHT OF

Nowadays, there are all kinds of special days and special weeks of the year, aren't there? In fact, there are lots of rather obscure ones which you might never have heard of. Perfect! Just what you need to attract the fiction editor's attention. Try Googling 'Special days of the year' and see what you come up with in terms of inspiration. For instance, one of my creative writing students wrote a short story for National Carers' Week from the point of view of the daughter looking after her elderly mother. But you could also do it from the point of view of the careworker or the mother herself.

SUMMARY

◆ Get your seasonal short story into a fiction editor's office, several months in advance.

◆ Try to think of an idea which will be different from anyone else's.

◆ Ask yourself what most people do on a certain day – and then think of what might happen if something prevented them doing it.

◆ Use the internet to find out about special days to write about.

EXERCISE

Pick a special day in the year and either write an outline for a short story or a complete short story. Keep it short – no more than 1,000 words. Make sure it has a plot with a problem that needs solving!

The following story appeared in *Best* for the Mother's Day issue:

—— Mother's Day ——
by Sophie King

I'm not looking forward to Mother's Day. In fact, I'm not quite sure how I'm going to handle it at all. In the past three years of Alice's short life, Mother's Day had been one of the big celebration days up there with Christmas and birthdays. You can tell how important they were from the cards she sent – with a little help from her father, of course.

I get them out now from the bottom drawer of the pine dresser where I keep precious things. Yes, I'm aware it's a bad idea but I can't help myself. There are only three of them but I know each one by heart. The first has a picture of a big fluffy rabbit, blowing kisses and the words 'To the best mum in the world'. I've often thought it was funny that so many cards say that. There must be an awful lot of 'bests' out there.

'Have a wonderful day because you're a mum in a million,' Alice had written although she couldn't really have done so because she was only a baby then. I remember that time so clearly. It seemed amazing that we should have a baby at all after all those false hopes and disappointments. Alice had arrived the week before Mothering Sunday which couldn't, as we agreed, have been better timing.

The second card is a pink, glitzy affair with ribbons round the edge. We always dressed Alice in pink because she had the kind of round face that might easily have been mistaken for a boy. Alice had been two then and she had managed a scrawl with one of those pink gel pens. If you use a lot of imagination, you could just make out the word 'Mum'. Instead of a rabbit on the front, there were lots of hearts surrounding a picture of a little girl, hugging her beaming mum.

She was a fast walker, Alice. It was all we could do to keep up with her, especially as we knew then that we were on borrowed time. That's why the third card is so special. It played a tune and I remember the first time I opened it, Alice was so entranced that she kept opening and shutting it to make the tune play over and over again.

'You'll break it,' I warned her but she just gave me a cheeky smile and carried on in her own sweet way. By now, Alice could write her own name which made all those hours with those flashcards, seem worthwhile. She also did her best with the other words although you'd have to know what they said to be able to decipher them. 'To Mummy,' it said. 'Thank you for being my mum. Love Alice.'

There should have been a fourth card but cards didn't seem important this time last year.

There was a knock on the door and I suddenly feel very stupid. I was like one of those old people you read about who don't get many Christmas cards any more. So they put out the old ones from years gone by, to make themselves look more popular. What would people say when they saw Alice's old cards?

They wouldn't say anything, that's what. They'd look away embarrassed and then change the subject the way that most people have done since it happened.

There's another knock on the door now. A more impatient knock. No guesses who that is. Quickly, I put the cards away and open the door. A small blonde bombshell tears inside, hugging my legs and then charges off into the lounge to turn on the television. 'Take your shoes off,' I call out but she ignores me as usual. You can see who the boss is round here.

'Hi.' Teresa, our childminder, hovers on the doorstep as though waiting for something. I don't know what I'd do without Teresa, especially in the holidays. She has Alice three mornings a week although I normally pick my daughter up from her house. Today, however, she asked if she could do this as she needed to 'drop something off'.

I look at the envelope in her hand and feel sick. She's going to hand in her notice. I'd been wondering when this would happen. For the last few years, Teresa has been doing her Open University degree and it was only a matter of time before she got a job outside the home.

'Can I come in for a minute?' She smiles awkwardly at me. 'I need to give you this.'

I step backwards. 'Please don't.'

'Why?' She looks alarmed. 'You don't know what's in it.'

'I think I do.'

'Really?'

And then I see that there are two envelopes. 'One's for you from Alice. She made it herself. And the other is from me.'

Alice has heard us talking and come rushing out into the hall, leaping into my arms. 'Open mine first, open mine.'

So I do.

'To the best mum in the world,' it says. And my eyes fill with tears.

'Can we put it with the others?' asks Alice brightly. 'The secret ones you usually keep in the bottom drawer? You could get them out so they don't get lonely.'

I nod, not trusting myself to say anything. Silently, I open the second envelope.

'Open the card, open the card!' sings Alice, jumping up and down.

So I do and it's exactly the same card as last year except that the Happy Mother's Day is crossed out and in its place, is written Happy Daddy's Day. 'It even plays the same tune!' says Alice. 'Weren't we clever to find it! It means you've got one just like mummy's.'

'The cards were Alice's idea,' said Teresa quietly. 'I hope you don't mind.'

'They're lovely,' I manage to say.

'Do you think mummy can see her new card from heaven?' demands Alice.

'I'm sure she can.'

'That's what Teresa said,' announces Alice cheerfully.

Then something flutters out of the envelope. Two little bits of paper. I pick them up. To my surprise, they're theatre tickets. I look at Teresa wonderingly. She's rather pink. 'I wasn't sure but I just thought...well if you're not busy that is...'

'Thank you.' I smile broadly at her as Alice grabs each of our hands and tries to swing herself forwards. And suddenly, Mother's Day looks a lot brighter than it did before.

(13)

Writing Serials

This is a short chapter because serials are a very specialised subject. A fiction editor once told me that it was much more difficult to write a serial than a short story. For a start, you need something that is going to sustain the reader and the fiction editor through four weeks or even more.

Each instalment is usually 2,000–3,000 words but can go up to 5,000 plus. That's quite a lot of writing! Some writers send in the whole serial together with a synopsis. Personally, I'd be worried about investing all that time unless I had a commission first. So my advice would be to outline an idea and write the first instalment. Then send it to a fiction editor, making sure it fits in with the guidelines.

Read other serials which the magazine has printed to check you're on the right wavelength.

Some magazines will ask you to write more instalments to see how it turns out. Do this even if there's no guarantee they will accept it. It shows they are interested.

PLOTTING YOUR SERIAL

Start thinking about a longer plot and characters which can develop over several weeks. What kind of problems will they have to face? Is there enough to keep them going? What are the sub-plots? In a serial, you will have time for sub-plots.

Serials can also be a good spot for historical novellas. Magazines like *The People's Friend* are often keen on serials which are set in the past.

I've just had a serial accepted by *My Weekly* but it was after several weeks of discussing ideas. If you're going to write a serial, be prepared for lots of planning and commitment; rather like a novel.

Finally, don't be disappointed if you don't have a serial accepted. Some writers find they can write short stories or serials but not both.

(14)

Are You Fit for Publication?

There's a great temptation when you've written your short story, to send it off immediately to a magazine or what every publication you've identified. After all, you've finished it, haven't you? And that's a great achievement, especially if it's the first you've ever written.

But stop! I mentioned earlier that writing a novel and writing a short story are both different and the same. And one of the similarities that both disciplines share, is that you should never send something off immediately without allowing it to settle in your head. I can't count the number of times I've thought I'd finished something and then another idea will occur to me within 24 hours.

If that story or novel has already been sent off, I can't ask for it to be sent back so I can make changes, without looking unprofessional. Far better to put it in a drawer for at least a week and then go back to it.

Not only might you add something you've thought of but the time gap will also give you a chance to look at it again with fresh eyes. You can check the grammar, re-read the story outline and make sure the pace is right from the exercises I gave you earlier in the book. In short, you can ensure it stands the best possible chance of getting published.

PRESENTATION

Professional presentation is essential in a short story (and novel). I can't stress how important this is. If a fiction editor opens an envelope to find a wodge of dog-eared papers which have quite clearly been passed around already from one publication to another, he or she is unlikely to jump on something which looks as though it's been rejected many times before.

It goes without saying that short stories have to be typed or word-processed. With word processing, there's no excuse for dog-eared stories. You simply print out another copy and make sure that any alterations are done beforehand so they don't look like additions to the piece. In other words, never write in an extra word or even a comma into a typed manuscript.

Each story should also be double-spaced and in a legible, readable font and size. I personally use Times Roman in 12 point or Arial in 12 point.

Make sure, too, that your name and contact number is on each page. This is because pages can be lost and it would be terrible if an editor liked your story but couldn't find the rest of it to see who wrote it.

Also put the word count at the end. This helps a busy editor who might think your word count is right but isn't quite sure.

Always post your short story instead of e-mailing it, unless the guidelines tell you differently. You'll recall from earlier chapters, that most magazines have individual guidelines for would-be short-story writers. The way in which a story is to be sent and any other advice is contained in these, so read them carefully. Don't assume an exception will be made for your story.

Some magazines ask for a stamped self-addressed envelope but not all. Again, check, the guidelines before wasting postage.

CHECKING YOUR MARKET

I know we covered this in the early chapters of the book, but I'd urge you to look at this again. Are you sure you're sending your story to the right market? Does that magazine still publish fiction? Does it still do a 'twist in the tale' series if that's what yours is intended for? If you're writing a seasonal story, are you sending it off at the right time of the year or is it too late? As I said before, you need to send it in at least two months beforehand if not longer.

WRITING AN ACCOMPANYING LETTER

Many of my students get very worried about sending off their first short story if they've never been published. 'Should I say it's my first?' is a very common question.

The answer is 'No'! You don't need to go into great detail about your background and how you got a good mark in English A-level but have never written professionally. It's your story which the magazine is interested in and whether it's pitched at their readers with the right word count.

Keep your letter short and to the point. You could say that you've studied the magazine's guidelines and would be grateful if the fiction editor would consider the enclosed. If you've won a competition, do mention that, however. Similarly, if you are doing a writing course and your tutor has said you have promise, you could mention that briefly too but don't make too much of it.

DO YOU NEED AN AGENT?

You don't need an agent for short stories. This is one of the pluses compared to writing a novel. Nowadays, very few publishers will consider a novel unless you have an agent because they reckon that if an agent if prepared to invest time and energy in you, you must have something.

However, the short-story market is different. From the writer's point of view, you're probably investing less time and energy in a piece of writing than if you were writing a 100,000-word novel. Similarly, a fiction editor of a magazine will use his or her own judgement, instead of that of an agent, to see if he or she wants your story.

Therefore you can go straight ahead and send that story off to a magazine without having to persuade someone in between that it's good enough.

One less hurdle to cross!

GETTING ORGANISED

Buy a large notebook and make a note of which story you're sending to which magazine. Write down the date and also the title followed by a brief outline of the story so you can remember what it's about.

Never send the same story to more than one magazine. It's the quickest way to annoy two publications if they both want it. Learn to be patient. Magazines can take at least two months to reply and they won't appreciate being hassled. If, on the other hand, you haven't heard anything after that, you're perfectly within your rights to make a polite phone call to the fiction editor and ask if they received the manuscript safely and how long they think they might need before making a decision.

Don't say 'I've got another magazine that might be interested' or they'll know you've sent it to someone else. Editors won't like this because it means they could be wasting time looking at something which someone else has already offered for.

Dealing with rejections

If you get a rejection, you're bound to feel upset. But learn from it. Sometimes, a fiction editor will be good enough to say why he or she didn't like it. Now's your opportunity for a second chance. Read the criticism even if it's just a sentence saying it was 'to predictable'. Was it? Swallow your pride and re-write part of it so it's less predictable. Perhaps you might like to change the title at the same time to give it a fresh look.

If the editor says it's too similar to something she's already accepted, take heart. This means you're on the right track. So send it to another magazine instead. But make sure you keep your records up to date by putting a rejected note next to the first and then writing down which magazine you've sent it to again.

IF AT FIRST. . .

One of the tips a writing friend gave to me when writing this book, is to encourage would-be short-story writers to send off stories regularly. 'It's no good writing a story every six months and then be disappointed when it doesn't get anywhere. The trick is to write one every week if you can and keep going.' (See tips on writing at the end.)

SUMMARY

- Don't send your story off as soon as you've finished it. Sit on it and then look again with fresh eyes.
- Check the guidelines of the magazine you're sending to. Have you followed them to the letter?
- Double space your work and ensure there's a contact name and number on each page.
- Make sure the manuscript is clean and tidy without pen marks.
- Always type or word-process your work.
- Only e-mail your story if the guidelines say you can. Otherwise, post it.
- Keep records of which story you've sent to whom and when.
- Allow two to three months for a reply.
- Never send the same story off to more than one magazine unless the first has rejected it.

EXERCISE

Take one of your short stories and follow the above guidelines. Make sure you're happy with the presentation and content. Then post it off to a magazine. Good luck!

Competitions

Competitions can be a great way of getting a short story published. They can also leave you feeling like a failure if you don't get anywhere, even though you were convinced your story had that special X factor.

The best way to treat competitions is as an experience. See it as an opportunity to use your talents and to be guided by the structure it offers, rather like a writing exercise. You're being told how many words to write and probably what subject to write about. If you get somewhere, that's wonderful. If you don't, you've completed a useful writing exercise.

HOW TO FIND COMPETITIONS

Certain magazines run regular short-story competitions. At the time of going to press, these include *The Lady, Good Housekeeping* and *Woman & Home*. There are also regular competitions in writing magazines like *Writers' News* and in writing organisations like the Society of Women Writers and Journalists.

You can find out about others by Googling the words 'writing competitions' or narrowing it down to 'magazine writing competitions'. As suggested in the previous chapter, be organised and write down which competition you've entered and which story you have sent in.

It's also well worth joining the Romantic Novelists Association. This valuable group of writers is for unpublished as well as published writers. It has nationwide events and also local meetings to encourage publication. The online arm (Romna) runs regular details of short story markets and competitions. You'll find contact details under Useful Contacts at the end of the book.

Some competition organisers charge a fee to enter. This might affect your willingness to enter.

MAXIMISING YOUR CHANCES

You wouldn't believe how many entrants are disqualified before their entries are even read, because they haven't followed the rules. So read the small print carefully! If you've had a short story published somewhere else, you might not be eligible. You will probably not be allowed to enter if you have a relative who works for the magazine.

Make sure you stick to the word count or your entry will be instantly disqualified. Also read the brief carefully so you're writing about the subject specified (if there is one). Make sure you send your entry in, within plenty of time. What a shame it would be if you missed out because yours was a day late.

Material also needs to be original – so don't send the same short story to two different competitions. If you were placed with both, you'd have a lot of explaining to do and your name would not be popular.

HOW TO MAKE YOUR ENTRY STAND OUT

Remember the section on ideas? I suggested you looked at an

ordinary idea from the bottom and the side and upside down. Pick it up like a box and see it from a different angle in order to find a way of writing a story that will be different from everyone else's.

This is one of the best pieces of advice I can offer when it comes to writing a short story so that yours stands out from the crowd.

Let me give an example. Some years ago, when Arthur Hailey was alive, I entered a short story in *The Lady* magazine which he was going to be judging along with Rosamunde Pilcher. The subject was about a mystery journey. Now it so happened that I'd recently returned from a trip abroad and been struck, as I always am, by the group of people in Arrivals who stand, waiting for people whom they don't know with their names on a placard or piece of card.

It made me wonder what would happen if someone pretended to be someone they weren't. After all, the person meeting them, might not know their true identity. But how could that happen? I based my story on an eccentric but loveable old lady from Australia (rather like my then husband's grandmother) who'd taken herself off on a trip round the world. When she got to the airport, she saw a family who were waiting for a distant great aunt whom they'd never seen. They thought she was the great aunt and who was she to put them right? She then spent a few days with them, before leaving just before the real one turned up (after being delayed).

But the interesting thing was that the fake great aunt had managed to get the family to stop arguing and to make the children help their mother more. In return, she sent them a much-needed cheque to thank them for their hospitality. It was different, Arthur Hailey assured me during the prize giving lunch (I came second). And that is part of the trick.

FROM THE JUDGE'S POINT OF VIEW

I've also been asked to judge short-story competitions. The experience has made me realise how important it is to do the following. I've already made these points but they're so vital, I'm going to do it again:

- ◆ Decent presentation.
- ◆ Interesting title.
- ◆ Contact details attached (for competitions, you might be told not to put your name on each page so the entry can be judged objectively).
- ◆ Readable font and point size.
- ◆ Unusual way of tackling the subject.
- ◆ Believable characterisation.
- ◆ Pacey plot.

PRIZES

Competitions can be worth entering for the prizes alone. These vary tremendously but the most useful are either money or the chance for a publisher and/or an agent to see your work. Some competitions also offer writing courses as prizes.

GOOD PRACTICE

Competitions can also be useful sources for ideas. You might find it gives you useful ideas for writing a story for someone else.

SUMMARY

- See competitions as a writing exercise. If you win, it's a bonus.

- Use competition titles as a source of ideas for your own work.

- Look out for different competitions. Keep a folder of forthcoming ones. Keep records of what you've entered.

- Never send the same story to different competitions unless you know you haven't won.

- Look out for competitions where the prize is linked to meeting an agent or editor.

EXERCISE

Find a current competition and enter a story. If you don't feel confident enough, use the title of an old competition as a writing exercise.

16

Money, Money, Money...

If this is the chapter you've turned to first, you might not just be reading the wrong book. You're quite possibly in the wrong field of work!

Although there are writers who make a mint from their writing – and surely I don't even need to mention names here – most of us are lucky if we can support ourselves through our work.

But there's more to it than that. If you're a real writer, you'd do it even if no one paid you a penny. In fact, I'd go further. I'd personally pay someone if I had to, just so I could write. I'm not talking about vanity publishing as I wouldn't go down that particular road myself. I'm talking about that need inside me to put pen to paper or, rather, fingers to keyboard.

For me, it's the writing which matters and not the cheques. And I'd firmly suggest that if you want to write, you have the same approach. Otherwise, you may well be disappointed and would probably be better off signing up for a highly-paid, highly-stressful sales job.

ON THE OTHER HAND...
On the other hand, if you are lucky enough to have a short story accepted, it's fair that you should be paid. So what can you expect to get?

This is a tricky one. To be honest, it often depends on the writer. A magazine might pay a new writer less until they've established herself or himself. Some publications offer more to established writers who have become a 'name'. They might also offer more to writers who aren't household names but who have sold several stories to that magazine already.

Not surprisingly, these rates are confidential and it wouldn't be worth blotting my own copybook to reveal what they are. However, as a ballpark figure, you could earn anything from £70 to £350 a story.

It's also worth approaching your local paper or free magazine give-away and offering to write a short story for free. It will help to build up your portfolio.

WHEN WILL YOU BE PAID?

Most magazines pay on acceptance although don't go spending it immediately you get the 'yes' letter! Payment can take at least a month to six weeks to come through.

Some magazines require an invoice. Others will put through the payment automatically. So check when you get that acceptance news.

SELLING ON

You can make money on the same story by selling it on, after publication. This depends a lot on the Rights Agreement you signed with the magazine. So always check with the magazine.

Even so, most magazines won't thank you if you sell on to another publication which has a similar readership. Nor will the new magazine. If you haven't told them it was published somewhere else, they would probably be very upset and rightly so.

There is a possibility that the magazine might not mind if the story had been run by a publication which was completely different. So my advice is to be honest at all times. Tell them where it was published before sending it off.

A much better approach, however, is to send it to a foreign magazine, especially in English-speaking countries, such as Australia or South Africa. Again, it's important to say it's been published in the UK and possibly to send them a cutting, showing how it was laid out. But you're more likely to be able to recirculate your work this way – providing it doesn't go against the agreement you signed with the British magazine in the first place.

Examples of overseas markets include:

Australian Woman's Weekly
Woman's Day in Australia
That's Life! in Australia
You in South Africa

Writers' News magazine also has a useful regular section on overseas markets.

SUMMARY

◆ Don't write for the money. If you earn, that's a plus.

◆ If money is important to you, concentrate on the markets which pay more. However, you'll be losing the opportunity to 'showcase' your work elsewhere.

◆ Consider foreign markets so you can sell on stories which have already been published.

EXERCISE

Take three magazine guidelines and look at what each is paying.

(17)

Writing Courses

How useful are writing courses for the would-be short-story writer? The answer is that they're as good as the course itself. And, of course, you won't know that until you invest the time and money to go on it yourself.

Even word of mouth can be unreliable. After all, what is one man's meat is another man's poison. Your friend might find a certain course useful for the kind of book she wants to write. But it might not suit you.

My advice is to shop around. Find out how much different courses cost and how often they run. Do they fit in with your lifestyle? Can you take two hours off a week to do a course or would you be better off with an online course where you can send in assignments to suit your own balance of hours?

Also, ask the organisers about previous students. Can you talk to them to see what they did or didn't get out of it? Did they get published? Also ask if you'll be assigned to a particular tutor. What is his or her background? If she's a specialist in sci-fi and you write contemporary romance, the two of you might not be a great match.

LOCAL AUTHORITY COURSES

Many local education authorities run creative writing courses. (I tutor one at the moment.) The courses tend to be reasonably priced but they will also attract a wide range of abilities. A good tutor will know how to keep everyone happy.

ONLINE COURSES

Organisations like the London School of Journalism (whom I also tutor for) run a variety of online creative writing courses which have nothing to do with journalism. For example, they run courses on writing children's fiction, adult novels and thrillers, amongst others.

The advantage is that you can submit assignments when it suits you (within reason).

UNIVERSITY COURSES

Some universities run creative writing courses for students who aren't undergraduates. At the time of writing, I am running a two hour weekly course for Oxford University, called Writing the Mass Market Novel. It lasts for 20 weeks. It's also possible for students to gain accreditation points during the course which will then count towards the beginning of a degree. For details, contact individual universities.

ONE-OFF WORKSHOPS

One of the most famous workshop organisations is the Arvon Foundation. There are also literary consultancies like Cornerstones which run weekend and one-day workshops. Alternatively, combine sun with creative writing with writing workshops abroad. (See the contact details at the end of the book.)

COST

This varies tremendously from course to course and it wouldn't be helpful to give you the cost of each one as they can change. As a rule of thumb, however, local authority classes are the lowest priced because they are subsidised.

CRITIQUES

There are several literary consultancies which offer individual critiques. These are mainly geared at novelists and can cost quite a lot. You could, however, ask if the consultancy would look at short stories too, although financially, you might not feel it is worth it even if your story then goes on to be published.

SUMMARY

◆ Do your research into writing courses. Prices and levels vary.

◆ Writing courses might be useful for some writers and not for others. This usually depends on the mix of students, the tutor's experience and ability, and what you hope to get out of it.

The Internet

I have to say that I'm one of those old-fashioned writers because I prefer to see my work printed on paper. But if you've tried to get published and haven't got anywhere, the internet can be one way of getting printed and will help you to build up your portfolio.

Start by Googling 'short stories' and see what comes up. When I did this, it threw up a variety of sites, some of which may not be there by the time this book is published. So it's best to do it for yourself and see what is available.

Do beware, however, of parting with money just to see your work published. This applies to all organisations and not just online ones. Vanity publishing, as it is called, is not always highly regarded by professionals, although it has a place for those who want to see their names in print and are happy to pay for it.

Also be aware that you have fewer controls over other people using your material from the internet.

COMPETITIONS
As I've already mentioned in Chapter 15, the internet can be very useful in sourcing competitions. It can also be very handy for researching your short story.

SUMMARY

◆ The internet can be an alternative to magazines and other forms of the printed word. But it may not be as long lasting and it can also be subject to plagiarism.

◆ Think carefully before parting with any money.

YOUR CHANCE TO GET PUBLISHED!

This is your chance to get published! Use the guidelines in this book to write your own short story. Send it to me at How To Books and I will personally select five to send to the fiction editor of a woman's magazine.

Tried and Tested Tips
from Writers and Editors

There's nothing like tips from the experts – including editors and writers. I asked the following for some advice.

Kate Jackson
(Short story writer.)

I always write a character sketch of the main character, e.g. appearance, family, likes, dislikes, etc. It helps me to get under their skin.

I also think in terms of dividing the story into introduction, middle and end.

Go on a short story writing course by experienced authors – I've also done courses with Sue Houghton and Lynne Hackles.

For *The People's Friend*, think – emotion, emotion, emotion. Does it tug at the heart strings? Make the reader feel something!

Is your ending too obvious – is there tension?

Put your story away for a week and look at it again with fresh eyes. I know it's hard to do, especially when you first start and are desperate to get a story out there. But do it anyway!

Read the magazines you're writing for, regularly.

Study the published stories in a magazine to get their style, i.e. *The People's Friend* stories are very different from *Take a Break's Fiction Feast.*

As soon as you've sent off a story start a new one.

Keep a note book for ideas.

Write visually. I like making up similes. (Images without the word 'like'. For example, the mirror moon.)

Get your small son or daughter to kiss the envelope for luck before dropping it the post box. Yes, I really do this.

Don't give up when stories are rejected. Try them somewhere else or rewrite.

Margaret Mounsden

(Short story writer. Published in *My Weekly, The People's Friend, Woman's Weekly* and *The Lady.* Winner of writing competitions.)

Eavesdrop shamelessly! Supermarket queues, charity shops are great places. I once listened to a whole conversation about shoes, went back to the car and while waiting for my husband, mapped out a story which I sold to *Woman's Weekly.*

Use all your experiences. A Sunday-morning visit to the council recycling centre resulted in a story sold to *The People's Friend.* I watched a young man coax his girl friend into eating crisps on the

Eurostar and used that scene in another story. Keep your eyes and ears open and try not to get arrested for loitering with intent.

Janet Gover and Lesley Eames

These writers recently gave a talk on short story writing to the London chapter of the Romantic Novelists Association. Lesley has written for *Woman's Weekly*, *My Weekly* and *The People's Friend*. Janet has been published in *The People's Friend*, *My Weekly* and *Yours*.

Short stories are a good way to use an idea that wouldn't necessary sustain a full novel. Writing short stories is also a great way to polish your writing skills.

Seeing one of your short stories in print helps overcome the rejection blues when you're trying to get a novel accepted.

What constitutes a good short story is very subjective. Janet illustrated this point by telling us that she sent the same story to the same magazine but it arrived on different editors' desks. One editor accepted it on the same day the other rejected it. A rejection from one magazine often goes on to be an acceptance from another. It's always worth bearing in mind that if there is a change of fiction editor, it's worth sending a rejection to the new one without saying it was rejected earlier.

Women's fiction magazines take a wordage from as little as 800 to 3,000, but anyone submitting a story should look closely at each magazine's guidelines. Thorough research is needed to target the magazine suitable for your story. The readers of short stories often have to fit in their reading around other life demands, which is why they might choose a short story for a train journey or before picking the children up from school, rather that choosing a full novel.

Elements needed for a novel include themes, characters, plot, setting, dialogue and conflict. The same elements are needed to make a 100,000-word novel but the craft is in knowing what to leave in, how to convey setting, background and character with the minimal number of words.

In a novel, you have two to three pages in which to hook the reader but with a short story, it's two to three sentences. The same applies to hooking the editor who will make the decision whether to buy.

Remember that an editor of a magazine receives several hundred manuscripts each week. However if an editor offers a suggestion for change, do it and then re-submit.

Just because the story has to be told in 1,000 words, doesn't mean it can't be exciting and fully rounded.

Magazines know their audience. Because of this, some elements of a story don't need to be explained as the readership would identify with the main character and understand their predicament immediately. For example, a young mother dashing through the school run or the bored housewife with awkward teenagers.

Short stories are mostly written by women for women and as such, a certain amount of cultural shorthand is permissible. This helps to minimise the words needed to give the story depth. Janet said that when she writes a short story she writes more slowly than when working on a novel as every word has to earn its place in a very tight word count.

Lesley says the key to a short story is remembering that the story is a slice of life rather than a whole life. The main character is at the point of change so backstory and superfluous detail should be dealt with selectively and economically. The short story writer has to hone his or her skill of knowing what to include, what to leave out, and how to be economic with words. One way to do this is to focus on the moments of change for the character. For example, if a character breaks her leg, we might not see her being rescued, or her trip to the hospital. However, a few short lines of dialogue and narrative will tell us all we need to know about the result of her accident.

Look out for readers' special publications such as *Fiction Special* and the Christmas and holiday reads. Plan ahead to submit stories in time.

Read the magazines you are targeting and analyse them. How many are written in the first person: how many are romances: how many involve family themes?

Most markets have very specific guidelines on what they want – and they do change from time to time. The important thing, therefore, is to stand out from the crowd with a gripping opening and a word count that meets the magazine's requirements. The same goes for the title, the theme and taboos (no sex before marriage for *The People's Friend*, for instance). Presentation should be excellent too.

Paula Williams

(Short story writer and columnist for Writers Forum.)

When I started writing short stories, I relied heavily on my family as a source of ideas. I'm one of six children and had a lovely, chaotic childhood which I still mine mercilessly (and exaggerate slightly! But hey, I'm a writer – it's allowed.)

The first story I ever sold was heavily autobiographical and I felt so bad about telling the world some of the things I made my unfortunate younger brothers do, that when the story was published, I bought each of them a box of chocolates, a bottle of champagne and a copy of *Woman's Weekly*. I'm not sure if they've forgiven me yet.

I still rely heavily on things that happen to me for ideas – it's all to do with the way you look at a situation, isn't it? It also helps to have a finely developed sense of the absurd. But when all else fails, I have a book (*The Writers Book of Days* by Judy Reeves) which contains a different prompt for every day of the year. I then take the prompt for the particular day (this stops me wasting time wondering which one to choose) then I write and write, without stopping to think, until something comes. And, surprisingly enough, it always does – eventually.

Linda Mitchelmore

(Short story writer for a wide variety of women's magazines.)

I don't do thriller, I'm afraid, and my mystery stories tend to be twist in the tale – the reader thinks it's her husband but it's her son and so on.

To get over writers' block, I use my five pot system. I have four pots marked: people, problem, place and plot. The fifth pot is marked emotion.

Into the people pot, I put bits of paper with names on, and sometimes jobs or status. Doing it like that if you have a favourite name for a heroine like Beth, for example, you can have Beth/dentist, Beth/single Mum, Beth/child whose mum has died and so on.

I fill the problem pot with all sorts of things...car broken down, can't find love, bailiffs are coming.

For places I might have supermarket, office, chip shop, motorway services. The plot is things my heroine might do to sort her problem – join a choir, learn to swim, hook up to online dating.

Emotions cover just about everything...fear, jealousy, sorrow, elation, envy...and some less common like empathy and humiliation. I take one piece of paper from each pot and a story is written around them. I add to these pots all the time (currently they are jam jars!) and pop new names etc., into them when I meet or read about someone with an unusual name or job or whatever.

I once met a man who gilded mirrors and he had real gold flake in his hair and I got a story that sold in the UK, Sweden and Australia out of that.

If something I send out gets rejected (we all get them), I often just send it straight out again somewhere else because I know there are lots of reasons for rejection – I might have written about dogs but the editor is a cat lover, and vice versa. I might have a really kind and nice male character but the editor has just been jilted, or conversely I've written a horrid male character and the editor is newly in love.

Also, the editor might have just commissioned/bought/published/ sent to press a story very similar to mine but she just doesn't have time to tell me all that. If that story is rejected again, I apply my scissors! That is, I cut the first third and start the story again a third in, sometimes feeding in the first third as backstory. Often doing this makes a whole new story.

Story still not sold? Then I might change the names, or the job, or the setting... again an entirely different story appears on my screen after a couple of substitutions – most things sell in the end, I'm pleased to say.

I also have a BOSS when discipline is lacking – Bum On Swivel Seat – nothing's going to get done if I don't sit down and do it...

Lynn McCulloch
(Short story writer.)

There's masses out there about technique, plot, character, etc., but I think there's one crucial point to make.

Magazine-type stories are a five- to fifteen-minute read. They will then, generally, be discarded. So – write it the best you can, put it on one side, polish it, send it off and move on to the next one. I've known, and taught, numerous people who write great stories, but only one every six months by the time they've finished tweaking them. This is no way to build either a career or a bank balance!

Jan Jones

(Short story writer published in most major women's magazines. Winner of the Elizabeth Goudge short story competition in 2002.)

Because a short story has limited word-length, a good title is crucial. It will set up a reader's expectation so that you don't have to waste words laying out the setting, or perhaps the plot or the theme, leaving you more space in which to concentrate on other aspects of your story.

For example, a story called 'To the Ends of the Earth' suggests travel, loyalty and deep love before you even start reading it. 'Remember, Remember . . .' tells the reader that what follows will be about Bonfire Night.

My Elizabeth Goudge winning short story was entitled 'Nobody Knits These Days', which says straight away that one of the main characters will be elderly and that the theme of the story is likely to be about good, solid values. The title is part of the story. A well-thought-out title makes the rest of the story easier to write.

In my view, naming is also a vital aspect of writing. Choosing the right name for a protagonist can imply age, background and character. Think of the different people implied by Catherine, Cath, Cat, Katie, Kitty and Kate (or even, these days, K8).

Or how about William, Will, Billy or Bill? All quite different. Using an evocative name negates the need to expend precious word-count on description. For example, Charles implies a straight-laced older middle-class man whereas a Wayne is likely to be younger, brasher and more down-market. Hilda is going to be at least in her seventies. Emmy-Lou will be American. A rose by any other name, in other words, just won't be so effective.

Woman's Weekly

We want our stories to portray up-to-date characters in believable modern situations. We welcome stories on a wide range of themes and moods, for instance, warm stories about children, teenagers and family problems of various kinds; love stories, funny stories and even stories with a crime or thriller element, so long as they are not violent, threatening or too incredible. In other words, fiction that grips the readers rather than sending them to sleep!

One of the main reasons we reject stories is that we can tell from the word go what their outcome will be. Unless there's an element of tension or uncertainty, readers won't bother to finish a story. And unless they can believe in the characters, they won't get involved in the first place. The best way to achieve this involvement is to be subtle in your writing. 'Show don't tell' is a useful maxim to bear in mind. And don't give away too much too soon. Tempt your reader on with more and more clues.

Useful Contacts

MAGAZINES

Best Magazine, 33 Broadwick Street, London W1F 0DQ. Tel: 020 7339 4466.

Candis, Newhall Publications Ltd, Newhall Lane, Hoylake, Wirral CH47 4BQ. Tel: 0844 545 8100.

Fiction Feast, H. Bauer Publishing, Academic House, 24–28 Oval Road, London NW1 7DT. Tel: 020 7241 8000. Fax: 020 7241 8056.

The Lady, 39–40 Bedford Street, London WC2E 9ER. Tel: 020 7379 4717.

My Weekly, The Fiction Editor, *My Weekly*, D. C. Thomson & Co. Ltd, 80 Kingsway East, Dundee DD4 8SL.

The People's Friend, The Fiction Editor, D. C. Thomson & Co. Ltd, 80 Kingsway East, Dundee DD4 8SL.

Take a Break, H. Bauer Publishing, Academic House, 24–28 Oval Road, London NW1 7DT. Tel: 020 7241 8000. Fax: 020 7241 8056.

Woman's Weekly, Blue Fin Building, 110 Southwark Street, London SE1 0SU. Main switchboard: 020 3148 5000.

Writers News, 5th Floor, 31–32 Park Row, Leeds LS1 5JD. Tel: 0113 200 2929. Fax: 0113 200 2928.

Yours, Media House, Peterborough Business Park, Peterborough PE2 6EA. Tel: 01733 468000.

Monthly magazines like *Good Housekeeping* also run annual short-story competitions.

WEBSITES

Romantic Novelists' Association www.rna-uk.org
Arvon Foundation www.arvonfoundation.org
Cornerstones www.cornerstones.co.uk

MISCELLANEOUS

Hilary Johnson Authors' Advisory Service, 1, Beechwood Court,
Syderstone, Norfolk PE31 8TR. Tel:/Fax: 01485 578594.
E-mail: enquiries@hilaryjohnson.com
London School of Journalism, 126 Shirland Road, Maida Vale,
London W9 2BT. Tel: 020 7289 7777. Fax: 020 7432 8141.
Writers Circles: provides details of courses, including those in the
sun. www.writers-circles.com

Index

accent, 93
agent, 167

baddy, 52
beginnings, 109–11

categories, 6–7
characters, 49–54
comedy, 10
competitions, 170–3
crime, 14

dialogue, 85–95
double meanings, 124

endings, 112, 113

feel-good stories, 132–9
first person, 99–104

ghost stories, 146
grammar, 90
guidelines, 6

humour, 7

ideas, 1, 27–35, 62
index cards, 64

internet, 182

letter, accompanying, 166

market, studying the, 1–26, 166
middle, in the, 114
money, 175
mystery, 146

occasions, 156
overseas markets, 177

pace, 66
paragraph game, 67
plotting, 62–8
point of view, 154
presentation, 165
publication, 164–9

reading it through, 68
research, 35

seasonal stories, 153
serials, 162–3
sex, change of, 155
sting in the tale, 121–5
story lengths, 5